The Complete Microlight Guide

Ann Welch

In the same series:

The Complete Windsurfing Guide
The Complete Cycle Sport Guide
The Complete Sailing Guide
*The Complete Hang Gliding Guide

*in preparation

Copyright © 1983 Ann Welch

ISBN 0 7158 0835 4 (casebound)
    0 7158 0836 2 (paperback)

First edition 1983

**British Library Cataloguing in Publication
Data**

Welch, Ann
    The complete microlight guide.
    1. Ultralight aircraft — Piloting
    I. Title
    629.132'521   TL710

    ISBN 0-7158-0835-4

Published by EP Publishing Limited,
Bradford Road, East Ardsley,
Wakefield, West Yorkshire, WF3 2JN,
England.

Design: Krystyna Hewitt
Illustrations: Douglas Hewitt

Photograph credits
Gerry Breen 3, 6, 10(t), 11, 67, 79, 91, 95,
118, 134, 142(tl,cl), 149, 150, 151
Pat Connelly 26(t), 59(b)
Brian Cosgrove 41(c)
Flight Line Magazine 30(r), 41(bc), 50(t), 57,
62, 78(l), 80, 81, 92, 105, 113(b), 121, 128,
156(t)
Len Gabriels 47, 113(t), 135(3)
Bob Harrison 23(r)
Huntair Ltd 12, 32(t), 34(tr), 41(l), 61, 69
Michael W. Kent 116
MBA Ltd 53, 57(t), 72
Philip Newell 152, 153
Ordnance Survey 123, 126
Katie Thomas 8, 13(b), 14, 15(bc), 17
22(tl), 26(br), 27, 30(l), 31, 38. 58(bl), 59(t),
63, 86(b), 90, 96, 98, 103, 106, 107, 109,
110, 115(b), 119(tr), 131, 142(bl), 154,
155(bl + br)

The author wishes gratefully to
acknowledge permission to reproduce the
photographs listed above. All other
photographs are by the author.

Printed and bound in Italy by Legatoria
Editoriale Giovanni Olivotto Vicenza.

The Complete
MICROLIGHT
Guide

Ann Welch

Distributed by
STERLING PUBLISHING CO., INC.
Two Park Avenue
New York, N.Y. 10016

EP Publishing Limited
EAST ORANGE, NEW JERSEY

Contents

5

Introduction: What is a microlight?

Nearly one hundred years ago flying began with very simple, slow, lightweight aircraft. The Wright brothers' 1903 aeroplane weighed 280 kg, flew at 45 km/h and was constructed in a few months — including many pauses for thought.

Trike, the lightest and most versatile of microlights.

Lilienthal's 1895 glider weighed only 20 kg, flew at running speed and took a few weeks to build. But, because pilots always want something better, designers have been, and are, under constant pressure to make aircraft that will fly faster — which inevitably means that they become heavier, sleeker, more complicated, and much more

expensive. For the pilot who flies for fun this process has a habit of going too far, particularly as regards his pocket; so when a new type of simple aeroplane appears on the scene it is not surprising to see it gain immediate popularity.

Although now a sport in its own right, it was hang gliding which allowed people who could not

Early powered hang gliders used a small 125 cc engine driving a propeller via a long shaft. Because the thrust line was so high they were unstable in pitch.

One of the earlier production microlights. The Eagle is slow, light, and safe, but its drag is high so it will slow rapidly without power unless the nose is put well down. Its glide performance is poor so it will not travel far if the engine stops, but it is a useful trainer for learning solo, and fun for local flying.

afford conventional gliding to get themselves into the air and learn how to soar on thermals. Now the microlight is bringing power flying within reach of thousands of would-be pilots — as well as many experienced ones — who cannot afford the cost of more conventional aeroplanes.

The idea of a simple 'microlight' aeroplane is not, of course, new. Throughout aviation history designers have, from time to time, produced very light, slow aircraft, but until now they have never become really popular. This was because 'old-fashioned' construction methods were very time-consuming, and because the low-powered engines that were available were either too heavy or insufficiently reliable. Now all that has changed.

The breakthrough came with the hang glider, when it was discovered that a perfectly satisfactory flying machine could be made from aluminium tubes and dacron (terylene) cloth. Then a few pilots began to fit a little engine on to their hang gliders so that they could take off from flat ground instead of climbing laboriously to a hilltop. Unfortunately, various aerodynamic problems showed up in these early powered hang gliders, though it did not take long for the solution to be found. This was to put the pilot and engine into

a framework below the wing, and to give it wheels so that the pilot no longer had to run to take off. Most microlights are still constructed from tubes and fabric and have been developed into good, simple aeroplanes, capable of making satisfactory cross-country flights. In September 1982 sixty-four microlights set off during the London to Paris competition to fly fifty kilometres across the English Channel, and sixty-four arrived in France.

In many countries only a simple pilot licence is required by the national aviation authorities to fly a microlight; in others no licence is needed but pilots have to work towards proficiency certificates issued by their Microlight Association. However, simple legislation is only possible if the microlight can be clearly seen to differ from an ordinary aeroplane. This is why the *Fédération Aeronautique Internationale,* which is the world body for the encouragement and control of sporting flying, defines a microlight as follows:

FAI definition
A microlight (ultralight) is a one- or two-seat aeroplane having an empty weight (W) not exceeding 150 kg and a wing area of not less than W/10 m^2 and in no case less than 10 m^2.

This means that a microlight must remain an aircraft of low kinetic energy, and because it is so light and slow it is inherently safe — provided, of course, that it is properly built and maintained. The definition is not used in all countries and some have added requirements for their own national use, such as limiting the fuel carried to 9 litres (2 gallons) or permitting only single-seaters. Some countries use the word 'ultralight' instead.

Although microlights are slow, and cold and draughty to fly, there is no shortage of people who find this sort of aviation attractive. Many airline pilots fly these little aeroplanes in their spare time; to them the pleasure is being in the fresh air and able to wander about looking at the countryside without having to fly on schedule to some distant destination. Experienced private pilots who have found conventional flying too costly or over-regulated, or both, have turned to microlights to revive the pleasures of their early days, perhaps in Tiger Moths. Finally, there are the newcomers, mostly young, who have always wanted to fly, but until now have had no opportunity.

Although many pilots prefer to fly their microlights from a friendly farmer's field instead of from an airport, it is not necessary to fly

only from grass. Wheels can be exchanged for skis and the aircraft flown from packed snow, or for lightweight floats and operated from lakes or a calm sea. There are also 'amphibians' which allow the pilot to take off from his home field and land on water. Some microlights (called *trikes*) have a hang-glider wing which can be detached from the framework carrying the engine and wheels. The pilot then soars for a few hours in ridge lift over a hill and at the end attaches the trike framework and flies himself home in his 'aeroplane.'

Travelling by road

Nearly all microlights are designed to be easy to dismantle so that they can be transported on the roof of an ordinary car. The two wings are rolled up and put in bags to protect them from rain and dust. This portability makes it easier to travel to meets or competitions without having to wait for good weather, and also to return home after dark. If the method of construction does not permit such portability a light trailer may be used. This can, of

The Mirage weighs only 84 kg (185 lb), cruises at 40 knots, and stalls at 19 knots.

The French Sirocco, 3-axis controlled, has a glass-fibre fuselage and roll-up wings. The span is 10.12 metres and empty weight 105 kg. The JPX engine produces 26 hp.

Microlight flying is a marvellous way to see the country. This Mirage has an optional 'cockpit' to give the pilot some protection from the airflow.

Microlight pilots prefer to fly from a friendly farmer's field, far away from towns. *Left,* Trike; *right,* Eagle.

The lightweight Eagle on floats. It is slow, cruising at 30 knots, but stalling at only 17 knots.

A Pathfinder can travel by road on a small car.

course, also carry camping gear or even be used as a simple caravan, so that the whole family can be involved in weekend flying expeditions.

Fitness to fly
Although microlight flying does not demand the same physical stamina as hang gliding, it is an energetic sort of flying and the pilot needs to be fit, with his muscles in good trim. If he is not he will quickly tire and his judgement in the air will deteriorate; no sensible pilot should put himself in this dangerous situation.

Few countries require a strict medical examination; more usually the pilot has to declare in writing that he does not suffer from any illness which could affect his flying, and he may have to have this declaration countersigned by his doctor. But, in the long run, it is up to the pilot to be responsible for himself. If he has a cold, or a hangover, or a sprained ankle, he should not fly until he is properly fit once more. If any prescribed drugs are being taken he must ask his doctor if they will affect his ability to fly.

Pathfinder airborne. The pilot in the fresh air is warmly dressed, wears a sensible helmet – and his altimeter on his wrist.

Top: You need warm clothes, and tough shoes or boots, since it is often easier to taxi with the feet.

Below: Boots need thick soles, as on some aircraft the pilot's foot on the nose wheel is the brake!

Cold

In many countries cold is a greater problem than heat for the microlight pilot, and proper attention should be paid to wearing good protective clothing if the flight is to last more than a few minutes. Thermal underwear as used by sailors, and skiers' trousers and anoraks are recommended. The big difficulty is to prevent cold air creeping in around the neck, waist, wrists and ankles. Gloves are often necessary, but they must permit deft operation of quite small controls, such as the throttle and ignition switch. Big mittens may be warm but are too clumsy. More and more microlights are being fitted with lightweight cockpits or cocoons to give the pilot some protection.

Shoes and boots must be checked to ensure that they will not slip off rudder pedals or catch in wires. Training shoes are suitable, although the soles should be thick since on some aircraft the feet are used for taxiing or braking!

Helmets

Most pilots wear crash helmets, but, although they give good protection to the head, they are not mandatory. In some aircraft with enclosed cockpits, where head movement is restricted, the risk of collision with another aircraft is greater than possible damage to

the head in a bad landing. It is most important that the pilot can see, and his aircraft be seen. If the helmet is not going to impede his vision, then it is sensible that the pilot should protect his head. If a motorcycle-type crash helmet is used it should be a good one and made to the correct specification. This is usually the case with hang-gliding or despatch-rider helmets bought from reputable suppliers. Helmets should not be painted or covered over with stickers as this affects their strength. If a helmet has taken a hard knock, even if it looks only slightly scratched, it should be replaced.

Cockpit harness
Some microlights are fitted with lap straps and some with full shoulder harness — as gliders have had for many years. This harness is not only safer but more comfortable when flying. If you later buy an aircraft of your own, check that it has shoulder harness.

It is sensible to wear a helmet, but it must fit well, and enable the pilot to keep a good look out in the air.

This pilot may have a good helmet, but his chances of seeing another aircraft in the air are small.

1. Types of microlight: shapes and sizes

For a long time aeroplanes have remained remarkably conventional in shape — high- or low-wing with an engine in front and a tail at the back. But recently microlights, and a few light aeroplanes such as the Rutan-designed Quickie, have appeared, which are not in the least conventional to look at. Some, known as Canards, have the tail in front, while others have a swept-back wing and no tail at all. Some have the propeller in front, and others have it at the back, pushing the aircraft along. When seen from the ground these different configurations appear to fly in exactly the same way as each other, but to the pilot they all have somewhat different handling characteristics, and sometimes a

bewildering variety of control systems. So, although a microlight looks a very basic aircraft which is slow and easy to fly, no pilot, however experienced, should assume that he will be able to control any microlight without a very careful study of its handling, and an extremely cautious approach to getting airborne. This is because most pilots are used to the controls of an aeroplane behaving in a certain way, and if they do not it is easy to become muddled when the instinct to make a certain control response takes over. The complete beginner, learning to fly at a school, may find it easier, since he does not have anything to unlearn.

The differences which exist at

If it is windy, trike wings can easily be removed and laid on the ground so that they will not blow away.

The wing can be attached easily by just one person. Note how the framework folds to facilitate this, and to make it easy to transport on a car.

Ready to fly. The pilot is using a recoil starter to get the engine going.

Trikes are controlled by weightshift using the hang-glider wing control frame.

Trikes taxi across wind by holding the into-wind wing low.

present will lessen as microlights develop, but, in the present new and enthusiastic state of the art, there are certainly many of them. The biggest, however, is the least important: the fundamental difference between the 'aeroplane' microlight and those derived from the hang glider — the trikes — is not likely to disappear, but it is completely obvious.

Trikes

The trike, as mentioned above, is a direct descendant of the hang glider, and consists of a framework 'fuselage' unit with engine, pilot seat, and undercarriage which is attached to a hang-glider wing at a single point. It is flown using the ordinary hang-glider control frame to manoeuvre by weight shift.

The principle of control by weight shift is that the pilot shifts his body weight in the direction he wants the aircraft to go; moving his weight forward causes the aircraft to dive and gain speed, while moving it back raises the nose and slows the airspeed. Moving weight to the left or right will turn the aircraft to the left or right respectively. To see this in practice take a model aeroplane or glider and balance it on a finger. If a small weight is now hung from one wing that wing will go down; remove the weight — or centralise it — and the

model will return to its initial level position.

To shift your weight for a dive, you pull the control frame towards you. Since this is braced rigidly to the wing, it has the effect of moving your weight forward. When you want your weight back — to slow up — you push out on the control frame, and the straightening of your arms moves your weight aft. To turn you move your weight sideways along the bottom bar of the control frame, and as the aircraft reaches the bank angle you want you return your weight to the central position, and the aircraft will turn steadily.

A trike has no rudder, not even a tail, so the rudder cannot be used

to help fly around a turn. What happens is that when the wing is banked it begins to sideslip down in the direction of the lower wing, and the aircraft starts to yaw in the direction of the turn. You then control the rate and continuity of the turn by maintaining a suitable amount of bank and the correct airspeed.

As would be expected, a trike is a little more cumbersome to control than the hang-glider wing on its own because the mass and drag of the fuselage unit are greater than that of the pilot alone; so the control inputs by the pilot need to be bigger. In addition there are the engine controls: ignition switch or key, fuel on/off switch and a throttle

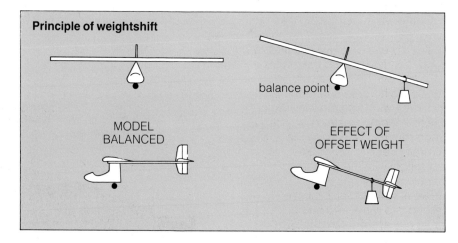

The principle of weightshift. The asymmetric weight causes the attitude of the aircraft to alter. When the weight is removed or centralised the aircraft returns to the original attitude.

for controlling the amount of power. The last should, of course, work in the conventional sense, i.e. forward for open (more power), and back to close the throttle.

Trikes are flown mostly by pilots who already fly hang gliders, or whose intention is to do so. For them the fact that the conventional 'aeroplane' microlight control inputs are different is of no importance. Some pilots fly both types without becoming confused, but only because they have converted from one to the other by small and easy stages until they can fly both instinctively — as indeed people have learnt to steer a boat, whose control inputs via the tiller are the opposite of those used in driving a car.

One advantage that the trike has over many other types of microlight is that it is easier to taxi in a strong wind. This is because the pilot is able to move his entire wing in relation to his fuselage, and can lower the wing into the wind which presses it down instead of getting underneath and blowing the aircraft over. An 'aeroplane' microlight with the wing fixed rigidly to the fuselage is near to the angle at which it will fly when taxiing into wind, and helpers may be needed to prevent the aircraft being blown over if the wind is at all strong.

The Eagle is also weightshift controlled. Here the pilot is pulling the bottom bar of the control frame in towards him, to move his weight forwards to increase speed. Movement of the pilot's weight also actuates the elevator on the canard to assist pitch control. The newer Eagle XL is controlled as a 3-axis aircraft with a stick.

The elevator on the canard can be clearly seen on this plan view of the Eagle. Also the sweepback in the wings to aid pitch stability. Remember, this Eagle is flying from bottom to top.

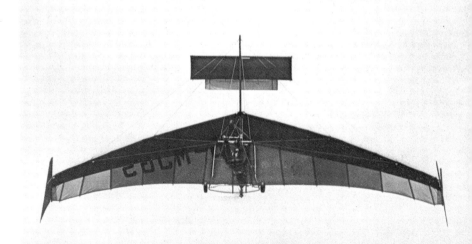

The American Quicksilver has no ailerons, and is turned using the rudder. This produces yaw which induces roll. The Quicksilver has been in production for many years and is available in a variety of versions, and different control systems. The latest version, the MXL, has spoilerons for roll control.

The Belgian Butterfly tandem wing biplane is the microlight version of the Pou de Ciel, or Flying Flea, of the 1930s. It weighs only 50 kg. It has no ailerons and the rudder is connected to the stick.

The British Dragon 2-seater has normal 3-axis control. Note the transparent panels to give an upward view for the instructor and pilot. It is one of the few microlights which is a 'tail dragger' and has a 'tractor' propeller in front, instead of a pusher.

The aluminium, mylar covered Lazair (Canada), has 3-axis control. It also has two 9 h.p. engines which drive biplane propellers.

The 'aeroplane' microlights

Many microlights look as though they are directly related to aeroplanes built before World War I because of their wire-braced structure and lack of cockpit. Fortunately they fly much better. The majority are of conventional aeroplane configuration with the tail at the back, although there is considerable variety in the positioning of the engine. There are two main advantages in placing it behind the pilot, as a pusher, and within any framework of tubes carrying the tail:

a the propeller slipstream does not blow all over the pilot as well as the airflow produced by his flying speed;

b it is not so easy for bystanders, and friends who should know better, to walk inadvertently into the propeller.

The disadvantages are:

a loose stones may be thrown up from the wheels during take off;

b engine cooling arrangements may be more complicated;

c some reduction in thrust may occur owing to obstruction caused by engine and pilot being in front of the propeller.

The aeroplane microlight is controlled in the conventional sense by a stick and rudder pedals, and is generally, though not always accurately, known as a 3-axis control aircraft. The three movements are:

pitch — nose up or down

bank — wing up or down (rolling the aircraft in the lateral sense), and

yaw — nose of the aircraft swinging to left or right.

The aircraft is turned using bank (left or right movements of the stick) together with yaw (left or right movement of the rudder) in the same direction as the bank.

Unfortunately some microlights are still not fully '3-axis'. Some use a stick to control pitch, but spoilerons or tip draggers to turn since they have no rudder. Others may have ailerons or spoilerons on the wings, and a rudder, but control pitch by weight shift using a sliding or swinging seat. A few even have a stick connected to the rudder with the rudder pedals controlling spoilerons on the wings for roll. This lack of standardisation is dangerous unless the pilot is fully aware of how the aircraft he is going to fly is controlled; the newcomer would be wise to buy an 'aeroplane' microlight only if *all* controls operate in the same sense as a conventional aeroplane. Apart from anything else it will be easier for him to convert to larger aeroplanes should he wish to do so at a later stage.

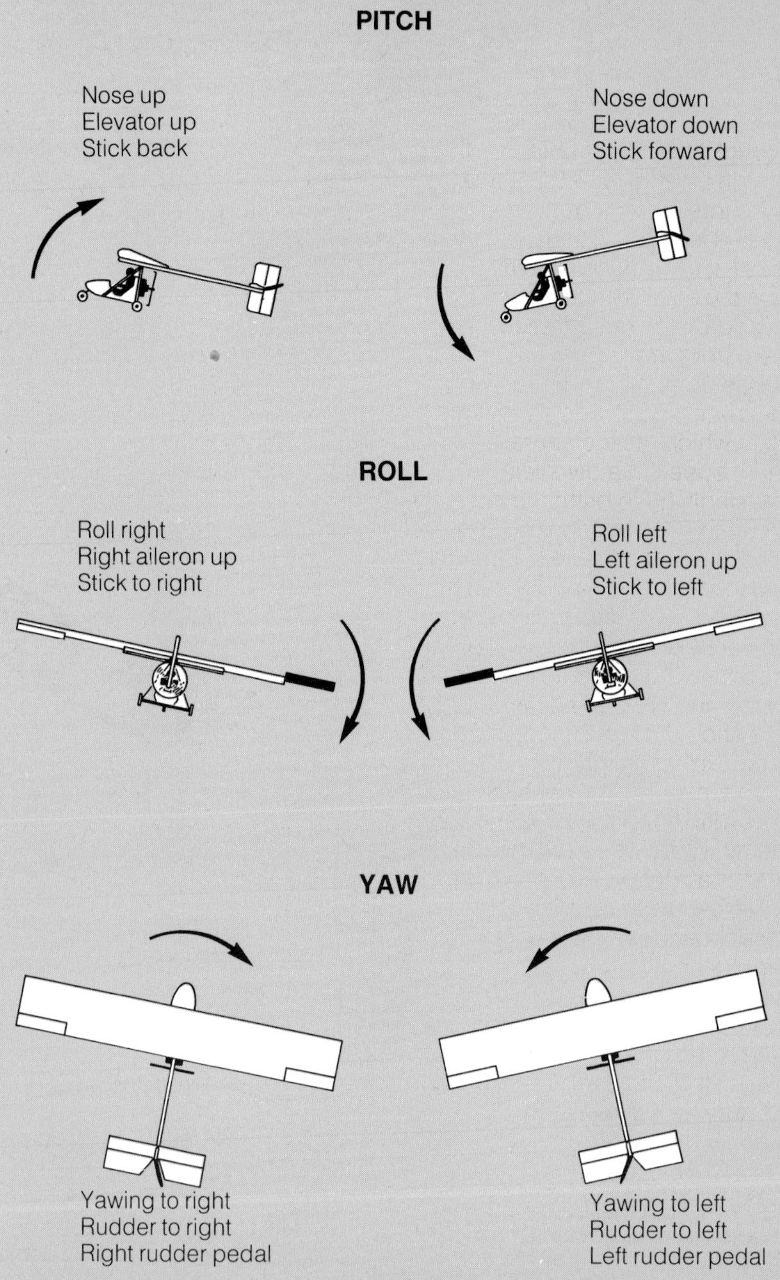

PITCH

Nose up
Elevator up
Stick back

Nose down
Elevator down
Stick forward

ROLL

Roll right
Right aileron up
Stick to right

Roll left
Left aileron up
Stick to left

YAW

Yawing to right
Rudder to right
Right rudder pedal

Yawing to left
Rudder to left
Left rudder pedal

Microlights without tails

Although an aircraft without a tail may be easier and cheaper to build and is easily transported on a car roof, it will not fly properly unless the stability normally provided by the tail is replaced by some other means.

This is done by giving the wing some sweep-back and a reflexed section which, as the aircraft gathers speed in a dive, will increasingly try to bring the nose back up to normal flying attitude. Without a reflexed section the dive would increase until the aircraft hit the ground. On wings which are floppy or flexible on the ground, like a trike wing, the reflex is held in by wires and shaped battens. These should *never* be adjusted or altered except strictly in accordance with the makers' instructions, otherwise the stability in the air will be affected and the aircraft may not pull out of a dive. On rigidly-built tailless aircraft reflex is built permanently into the wing.

A tailless aeroplane can be designed to have the stick and rudder operating in the normal sense so that the pilot flies it in the same way as if it had a tail.

Tailless aircraft need a reflexed wing section. As speed increases in a dive the reflex acts increasingly as an elevator, which raises the nose of the aircraft.

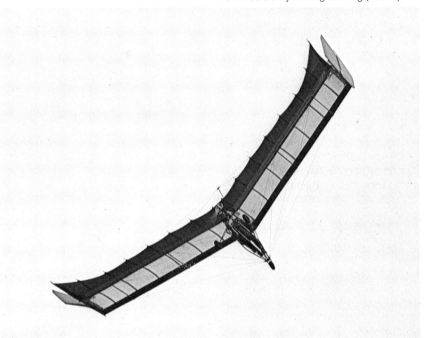

The Kasparwing swept tailless (USA). Lateral (roll) control is effected by ingenious wingtip rudders. It has been designed not to stall, descending more like a parachute if flown too slowly. It weighs 72 kg (160 lb).

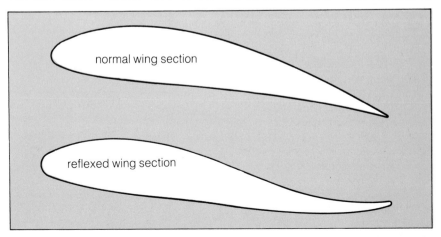

normal wing section

reflexed wing section

The Pterodactyl was developed from the Fledge hang glider, and has several variants including some fitted with a canard. It weighs 73 kg (175 lb), cruises at 35 knots, and stalls at 21 knots.

Canards

Some microlights — and other aeroplanes — are designed with the 'tail' in front. This can give the pilot a better view, and make the craft less likely to blow over on the ground. The canard surface in front is used for pitch control with, usually, tip rudders or draggers as the primary turning agent. As with a tailless aeroplane there is no reason why the controls should not operate in the conventional sense.

All this may sound very complicated, but there is no need for the newcomer to become an aerodynamicist to fly a microlight. If you want to involve yourself with hang gliding or just fly in the simplest way the trike may give you all you want; but if your intention is one day to fly bigger, faster aircraft, you should make sure that the aircraft on which you learn has its controls working in the normal aeroplane sense. This includes steerable nosewheels; if you push with your left foot the aircraft should turn to the left on the ground — *not* right.

Control movements
(Direction of movement at trailing edge of surface)

Cockpit control	Conventional 3-axis	Specials
Stick forward	Elevator down	Up on Canard
Stick back	Elevator up	Down on Canard
Stick left	Left aileron up Right aileron down	Spoilerons, left surface up
Stick right	Right aileron up Left aileron down	Spoilerons, right surface up
Pedal pushed left	Rudder left	Tip dragger, left dragger to left
Pedal pushed right	Rudder right	Tip dragger, right dragger to right
Elevator trim tab lever forward	Tab up	
Trim tab lever back	Tab down	

The AN–21–R is also a canard, with even more pronounced wing sweepback. This is a faster, more efficient aircraft with a glide ratio (engine off) of 18:1.

The Goldwing is heavier and faster than the average microlight cruising at 55 knots with a maximum speed of 75 knots. The stall speed is 23 knots.

Roll control on the Goldwing is achieved with rudders on the wing tips.

The Goldwing wings have slight sweepback and the canard has a high-lift-section fixed part with a narrow elevator for pitch control.

2. Controlling a microlight

The wing

A microlight flies like any other aeroplane in that it needs sufficient airflow over the wings to enable them to produce enough lift. To achieve this airflow the aircraft has to move through the air at more than a certain minimum speed. The speed at which it travels through the air is called its *airspeed* and the slower speed at which the wings will cease to provide enough lift to support the aircraft weight is called the *stalling speed*. Speed through the air can be provided either by the engine, or if the engine stops, by gravity — gliding down towards the ground.

The wing is shaped in such a way that air flowing over it produces lift by creating low pressure above the wing and higher pressure below it. The amount of lift produced depends on the angle at which the airflow meets it (*the angle of attack*), and the speed at which it is moving through the air. (The angle of attack should not be confused with the *angle of incidence*, which is the angle at which the wing is mounted on the fuselage.)

An aircraft flying fast has the wing at an angle of attack of only a

few degrees, whereas one flying slowly has the wing at a higher angle. The slowest speed at which an aircraft can fly is determined by the highest angle of attack at which the wing can produce lift without the smooth airflow over it becoming turbulent, usually about 15°.

Because microlights have plenty of wing and weigh very little their stalling speed is low — for a trike as little as 20 knots. Most microlights will fly safely at 4–5

knots above the stall speed, but with the throttle open will cruise at anywhere between 35 and 60 knots, depending on the type, and the power of the engine. All aircraft also have a speed above which they should not be flown. This is known as the *maximum permitted speed* or *Vne*, or sometimes *'redline' speed*. It is usually about 50 knots for a trike, going up to perhaps 70 knots for a Goldwing or Pathfinder. However, since few microlights have airspeed indicators, let alone ones calibrated for accuracy at the high

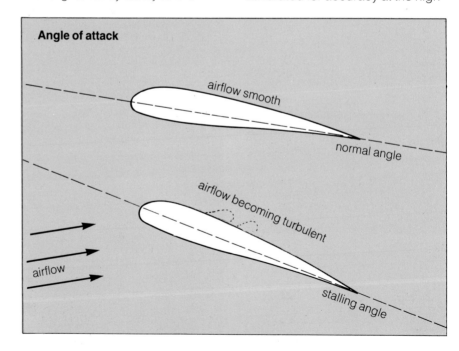

Angle of attack

airflow smooth

normal angle

airflow becoming turbulent

airflow

stalling angle

end of the scale, you should not attempt to find out by experiment how fast your aircraft will go. Generally microlights are not designed for aerobatics and you should not indulge in them unless the Permit or Airworthiness certificate specifically allows them. Any aircraft can be designed to be aerobatic but the necessary additional strength can come only from extra structural weight, and this is not the purpose of the microlight. It is intended to be an aircraft which is lightweight, slow, cheap, safe, and fun to fly.

Dihedral assists stability in roll (lateral stability). If a gust pushes up one wing the aircraft starts to slip. The raised wing has less lift and sinks until the lift on both wings is equal.

Stability

Aircraft are designed to be stable in flight. This means that if you let go of the controls the aircraft will either continue to fly steadily or will return to level flight. Any aircraft which, when left to itself, starts to dive or bank increasingly steeply, is unstable.

The designer goes to a great deal of trouble to ensure that his aircraft will be stable. He gives the wings *dihedral* to help it return from banked to level flight in gusty air.

He also designs the aircraft to be stable in pitch, so that it will not dive or stall of its own accord, although it will only remain stable in pitch if the pilot keeps within the c.g. (centre of gravity) limits.

Centre of gravity (c.g.)
The c.g. of anything is the point on it at which the resultant force of gravity acts. For example, the c.g. of a rod is halfway along it, i.e. the point at which it balances. The c.g. of a microlight, which has its wheels low down, its wing high up, and the pilot and engine in between, is somewhere under the wing. The exact position can be found by weighing or balancing the aircraft at a known attitude (usually with the top line of the fuselage horizontal).

In flight it is the position of the c.g. in the fore and aft sense which is important; with the aircraft reasonably loaded with pilot, fuel, etc, it should fly steadily, hands off, at normal speed and in all senses be easily controllable.

All aircraft are designed so that if

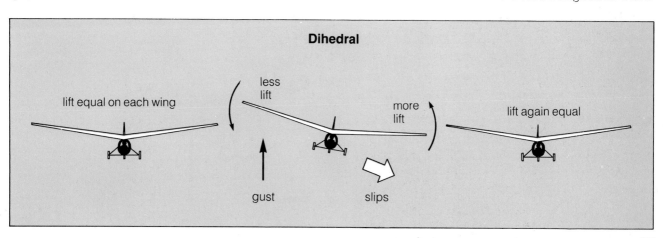

Dihedral

lift equal on each wing

less lift

more lift

lift again equal

gust

slips

The CGS Hawk. It is climbing at a steep angle of attack on full throttle. If the engine failed it would rapidly stall unless the nose was quickly lowered. It is unwise to climb at a steep angle close to the ground.

they are stalled the nose drops, thereby allowing airspeed to be regained. But if an aircraft is loaded incorrectly, with the weight of the pilot or his equipment too far aft it will be unstable, easier to stall, and more difficult to control. If the c.g. is too far forward the aircraft will be difficult to land. If the pilot is too heavy the stalling speed will be increased and the aircraft structure overloaded. So it is important that you always fly your microlight within the limits of its permitted c.g. range and cockpit load.

Trikes have generous wing area. This is about 15.3 m² (160 sq.ft). The sweepback is pronounced. Turns are produced by roll-induced yaw.

Spoilerons. The pilot is returning to level flight after a left turn.

Drag

Aircraft designers try hard to make a low-drag aircraft so that it will fly faster for less horse-power. Drag cannot be eliminated and there are two sources — *profile drag* and *induced drag.*

Profile drag is that caused by the shape of the aircraft itself. Many microlights produce a great deal of drag as the airflow makes its way past the exposed pilot, wires and tubes, and a wing on which the skin friction is high. Profile drag depends on the square of the speed, e.g. if the drag is 16 kg at 25 knots it will be 64 kg at 50 knots. This means that you will use much more power — and fuel — if you fly near your maximum speed than if you fly at the slower economical cruise speed. So, if you are getting short of fuel in the air, slow down as much as is practicable for the conditions.

Induced drag is that caused by the wing itself in producing lift, and occurs mainly at the wing tips when the higher pressure under the wing and the lower pressure air above the wing come together and create vortices. On a big aeroplane these vortices are so large and powerful that they will invert smaller aeroplanes flying in their wake — the well-known wake turbulence. Wingtips can be designed with

winglets or tip plates to reduce induced drag, but only slightly.

Induced drag is less at high speed, because the wing produces lift more efficiently, e.g. if the induced drag is 16 kg at 25 knots it will be 4 kg at 50 knots. From this it will be apparent that all aircraft have a speed at which the

total (profile and induced) drag is at a minimum. On a powered aircraft it is the speed at which the power required for level flight is least. On a glider it coincides with the speed at which the maximum glide is obtained. Should your engine stop it is useful to know what this speed is on your aircraft.

Performance

Microlights will take off after a very short ground run so they do not need an airfield from which to fly. In fact, an airport with concrete runways is undesirable as you should take off and land precisely into wind, and runways cannot be moved to suit!

On a smooth, dry, grass surface a light single-seater trike will take off in 25 – 50 metres, but more important is the rate at which it will climb having left the ground: there is no point in getting airborne if the aircraft will not clear trees at the end of the field. To safely use a field the size of a football pitch surrounded by the usual mixture of hedges, trees and telephone wires you need to be able to climb at about 500 feet per minute. If you go up at only 250 ft/minute the field will need to be almost twice as long.

If a farmer lets you use his field and no one has flown from there before you should carefully walk all over it, particularly where you expect to take off and land, looking for holes, rocks, etc. If the ground is soft or muddy, the grass long, or there is an uphill slope, your take-off run may be considerably longer; a combination of these things may mean you will not get off at all. Your take-off run will also be longer if the field is appreciably

higher than sea level or if it is a very hot day. The effective altitude, when high temperature is combined with height of the airfield above sea level, is called the *density altitude.* As it increases engine horsepower decreases, and the propeller becomes less efficient. This lengthens take-off distance and decreases the rate of climb. For example, if the height of the airfield is 4,000 feet above sea level and the temperature is 80°F (28°C) the length of the take-off run is doubled.

If there is any wind you should always take off directly into it, as it reduces the length of your take-off run by helping you reach flying speed sooner. When you come in

to land the wind against you effectively steepens your glide path and reduces your landing speed in relation to the ground. Your *airspeed,* however, must always remain above that minimum necessary to fly if you do not want to drop unexpectedly out of the sky.

When approaching to land on a gusty day you must give yourself extra airspeed, perhaps up to 10 knots more than you need in calm weather, since gusts and wind gradient (surface friction slows the air close to the ground) have a decelerating effect. And do not forget that should the windspeed against which you are flying be the same as your airspeed you will

The difference between airspeed and groundspeed. If you turned downwind your groundspeed would be 65 knots, but your airspeed would still be 50 knots. Do not become confused and mistakenly reduce airspeed.

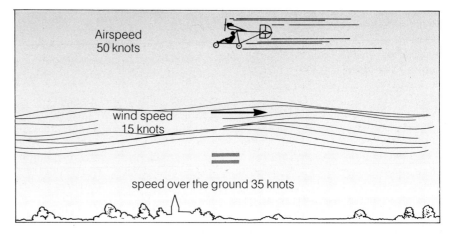

make no headway at all and never reach the landing field. If this seems to be happening you must increase your airspeed.

Because of its slow speed a microlight performs better and is more pleasant to fly in light winds and smooth air. It is affected much more than a heavy aeroplane by turbulence, down-draughts, etc, and not only because you are flying in them for a longer time than with a faster aeroplane. Equally, of course, a microlight can take greater advantage of thermals and the upflow of air over hills than its faster counterpart.

To obtain better climb rates and higher speeds some owners install a more powerful engine, going up from 30 hp to perhaps 40, but this should not be considered without much thought and technical

As an aircraft descends close to the ground, it flies into the lesser windspeed relatively suddenly, and temporarily loses energy — and airspeed.

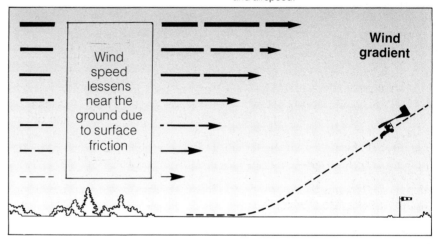

Wind speed lessens near the ground due to surface friction

Wind gradient

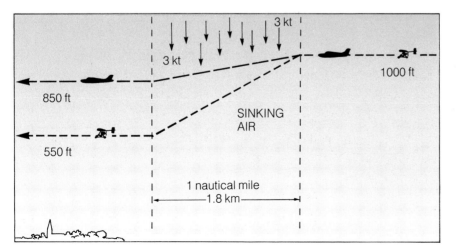

3 kt

3 kt

1000 ft

850 ft

550 ft

SINKING AIR

1 nautical mile
1.8 km

The aeroplane flying at 120 knots passes through the area of sinking air in 30 seconds and in doing so loses 150ft. The microlight, flying at only 40 knots, is in the sinking air longer — for 1½ minutes — and loses 450 ft.

Trikes have a short take-off run and need only small fields. As speed is gained the wing's angle of attack can be increased independently of the 'fuselage' and wheels, so take off can be effected immediately the wing is ready to fly — usually at about 18-20 knots. The pilot is pushing out on the control frame and moving his weight back thereby increasing the angle of attack.

advice, since the aircraft will be heavier, will need structural alterations and may not be as pleasant to fly.

3. Design, construction and materials

It is practicable to consider the structure of microlights in two parts: the wing; and the engine unit. This is because the construction and materials used for each part may be very different, and because on many trikes the wing can be detached and used as a hang glider.

The wing

Because the wing produces lift all the way along its span but has to carry the fuselage weight (pilot, engine etc.) centrally, the main loads on it are in bending — the tips want to bend up. In addition the wing has to resist torsion (twisting loads), because when flying slowly the air loads act more towards the front (leading edge), and when flying fast, further back towards the rear of the wing. In the air the wing is also subjected to drag loads — which want to fold

The Hummer. Note the bracing wires running from the king post to the top of the wing. These take landing loads, but in a gust may temporarily have to carry flying loads. The wires from the undersurface of the wing to the bottom of the 'fuselage' tubes are the flying wires.

Static testing for strength. This wing is loaded with 2000 kg.

the wings back when the aircraft is accelerating — so it has to be strong enough to resist these as well.

There are many ways in which wings can be made, but the most common at present is the tube and dacron construction. On a microlight, such as a Pathfinder, the wing has two aluminium tubes, the *spars*, one at the leading edge and one near the trailing edge. Such spar tubes are typically 50mm diameter with a wall thickness of 2mm. To prevent the wings bending upwards in flight flying wires run from them to the bottom of the fuselage on each side, while to hold the wings up when the aircraft is on the ground wires run from the top of the wings to a kingpost on top of the fuselage. On some microlights the landing wires are eliminated and the flying wires exchanged for tubular struts which can take both tension in flight and compression when on the ground.

Wing torsion is normally taken by spacing the flying and landing wires chord-wise on the wing. When flying slowly the front flying wires take most of the load, while

Landing wire tension can be slackened for de-rigging by sliding sleeves up towards the top of the kingpost. This is unsatisfactory as it reduces the torsional stiffness of the wing if it is subjected to negative loads in flight.

when flying fast the rear wires take more load. Inside the wing there is, of course, some structure to keep the spars and the wires correctly spaced, to give the wing the correct profile (wing section), and to resist drag loads. This structure normally consists of ribs, diagonal bracing, battens, and on some aircraft a faired leading edge. The popularity of aircraft which can be carried on a car roof complicates the structural problems since the various members will need to be disconnected or folded.

The wings of an aircraft are designed to withstand, without breaking, about six times the load they have to carry in normal flight. If, for example, your microlight flies at an all-up weight (including you) of 250 kg the structure should actually be capable of carrying a total of 1,500 kg, or 750 kg on each wing, before it breaks. This 750 kg load is spread more or less evenly along the wing, tending to bend it upward at the tip and upwards between the flying wire attachment points and the fuselage. It is the wing spars which take this bending, and the flying wires which prevent the wings hinging upwards.

From this it will be seen that the wing and its bracing need to be:
a properly designed,
b constructed of good quality materials, and

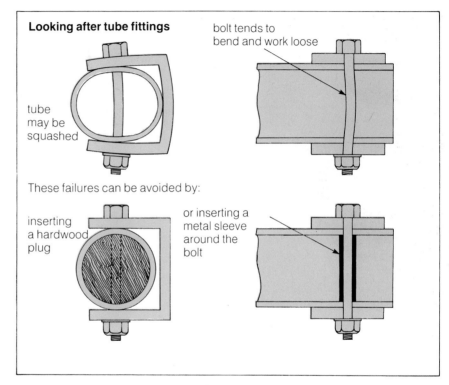

Looking after tube fittings

tube may be squashed

bolt tends to bend and work loose

These failures can be avoided by:

inserting a hardwood plug

or inserting a metal sleeve around the bolt

c not allowed to deteriorate.

Should it be necessary to replace a tube, a wire, or a bolt, on any part of your aircraft, it is *essential* that these are of the correct specification and size. Cheap, shiny bolts or any old rusty ones *will not do* if you value your life.

Unfortunately there are still some microlights around which were not very well designed, and contain features which are potential sources of trouble. In some cases structural or control members are joined together in such a way that they are under bending loads as well as tension or compression; in others, the load on a bolt is taken out on one side of the tube only. Another fault is to put bolts through tubes without fitting a block or sleeve inside the main tube, so that when the nut is tightened on the bolt the tube is squashed. Look carefully at lugs or tangs to which

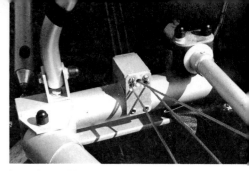

The homebuilt Resurgam. The wood construction permits a smooth surface and a well-shaped cockpit with protective windscreen.

Good workmanship but poor design of the control cable fairlead block. The cables will soon fray moving round such sharp bends.

The optional cockpit on a Pathfinder, comprising a glass-fibre nose dome with fabric sides and base. It improves the cruise speed by 4–5 knots over the completely open version

The glass-fibre Pipistrelle. The fuselage is moulded in two halves which are then stuck together. Glass fibre provides smooth and elegant aircraft, but it is not easy to make them light.

the ends of bracing wires are attached. Sometimes the direction of pull of the cable is offset so the fitting is subjected to excessive bending, and you may also find that the bend radius of such fittings is too sharp.

It is easy to say that you are only interested in flying, but failing to find out how your aircraft is made, whether it is strong enough, or how to maintain it, could result in problems. Although you may not be a qualified engineer, if you want your aircraft to be safe in the air, it is up to you to find out as much as you can about it. Chapter 6 tells you how to look after your own aircraft.

Other constructional materials

Although the 'tube and dacron' construction is light and basically simple, there are several other satisfactory materials from which microlights can be built, some being better for one-off homebuilts and others for factory production; glass fibre is a good example.

Glass-fibre microlights
Glass fibre is the standard material for high-performance sailplanes and can be used for microlight construction, but the problems of

keeping within the weight limitations are considerable. A simple shell can be made for the fuselage, with a tube for the tailboom, but the wing is more difficult. It can be made of solid foam covered by a skin of glass fibre (Goldwing), have a D-nose leading edge spar with fabric covering for the rest of the wing (Pipistrelle), or be a skeleton structure of spar and ribs covered with fabric (Duet). None of these methods is suitable for a 'roll up' wing. However, if a trailer — or a hangar — is used for storage, the glass-fibre method is attractive, as the maintenance is likely to be lower than for tube and dacron construction. The disadvantage is in the fragility of the wing if it strikes bushes or other obstructions. It is difficult to find out the extent of any damage, and the repair may be complicated.

It is bad practice to use a flexible paint on a glass-fibre structure since this makes the detection of hair cracks almost impossible. Repair of glass structures is more difficult than their manufacture, and it is essential to know what type of cloth and resin were used originally and to work to a repair scheme approved by the manufacturer. Most aircraft use epoxy resin for both laminating and

The glass fibre fuselage of the Duet. It is made in two halves and bonded together. The red knob is the throttle lever.

sticking components together. Some use polyester for laminating and epoxy for bonding. Using polyester as a glue, or laying up a new laminate on top of old polyester, is not satisfactory.

The greatest benefit of glass fibre in aircraft manufacture is that it produces a clean, low-drag aerodynamic shape with an excellent surface finish.

Wood

There is a sixty-year tradition of building lightweight aircraft structures in wood and thin plywood, and it is an excellent method for the home builder with skill and time who wishes to construct a single aircraft. The structural members are usually of spruce and can be quite small, e.g. girder-type ribs have been made of strips only 4 mm × 4 mm in section, with plywood coverings of only 0.8 – 1 mm thickness. This thin ply is normally of birch or beech though slightly thicker ply of gaboon (a lightweight, mahogany-like wood) is often used. Modern synthetic two-part glues give long-life structures. The normal wing consists of a spar with a D-nose of thin plywood. Fittings are normally made of welded sheet steel and the structure covered with very lightweight fabric.

This method of construction may be used for the whole aircraft, or for

The tail of the aluminium Lazair. An inverted vee tail is not usual, but here has been given small wheels to aid taxiing. The aluminium tube structure is covered with mylar.

the wing and tail surfaces only.

Steel tube

Surprisingly enough, a steel tube structure can be very light since it is possible to use thin tubes of quite small diameter. It is not suitable for a wing, but excellent for a fuselage when a pylon-like space frame is wanted. Normally 3–4 longerons are used with vertical and diagonal members connecting them. Considerable skill is needed in making the jig and cutting and profiling the ends of the tubes, but the welding by a skilled craftsman is quick. Here again fabric is used

for covering, although usually with some light wood members or strips to give the skin a fairer, smoother shape.

Aluminium

Aluminium is an attractive material since, unlike glass-reinforced plastic which has to be made specially, it can be purchased in large sheets. It is appropriate for the wing: e.g. a spar and D-nose of 16 thou. (0.016 in) thick aluminium is used on the Lazair which has transparent mylar film as a wing covering, giving a weight of only 64 kg for the aircraft. A disadvantage

The Lazair wing. The spar and central diagonal bracing is made up from sheet aluminium and pop rivetted. The ribs are of foam. The mylar skin makes inspection easy!

of aluminium is the difficulty of doing good rivetting with a very thin sheet, and while adhesive bonding is possible under controlled conditions, it is difficult for the home builder to be sure that his bond will be good enough.

Another disadvantage of any sheet metal construction is the need to have access to metal-working tools such as guillotine, bending rolls, brake press, etc. However, if these are available work can proceed quickly. It is a good construction material for use in a small factory.

The engine

2-stroke or 4-stroke

The engines used in practically all motor cars and conventional light aircraft are of the four-stroke type. They are called four-strokes or 'four-cycle' engines because four strokes of each piston (two up-strokes and two down-) are needed for each firing cycle.

In contrast, most boat outboard engines, and practically all those in microlights, are of the two-stroke type, where a firing cycle takes only two strokes of the piston, i.e. once every revolution of the

crankshaft. This is achieved by making use of the underside of the piston and the crank-case as a pump for sucking in the fuel/air mixture and pumping it into the cylinder.

Compared with four-stroke engines of the same power, two-strokes are lighter, more compact, smoother running and cheaper. But they are noisier, more temperamental and they use more fuel. At the present state of microlight development the advantages clearly outweigh the disadvantages; but it seems likely that four-stroke engines will gradually come into use, as quietness, low fuel consumption and long life between overhauls are important.

You can distinguish between a two-stroke and a four-stroke engine by looking at the cylinder head; if it is simply shaped, with the sparking plugs placed over the ends of the cylinders, it is a two-stroke. A four-stroke has the sparking plugs placed at an angle between the boxes containing the valve mechanism.

Engine layout — 2-strokes

There are many different types of engine in use, with one, two, three or four cylinders, and with wide variations in design. The cylinders can be arranged in an upright or inverted position, radially, or in the

The 250 cc Fuji Robin mounted on the Hummer. The reduction drive with 3 vee belts can be clearly seen.

flat configuration. Since a single-cylinder engine is inherently rough running, there is increasing interest in two-cylinder engines. Here the two cylinders are normally arranged to fire alternately, which gives more even power and, because the pistons are moving in opposite directions, better balance. (Some small, horizontally-opposed twin-cylinder engines are an exception, with the pistons moving in opposite directions to ensure good mechanical balance but with the cylinders firing simultaneously.)

Unlike the lubrication system of a four-stroke engine where the oil is circulated around the engine by means of a pump, two-stroke engines are lubricated by simply mixing some oil in with the fuel. As a result the engine can be mounted any way up without difficulty. In some installations it is more convenient to have the crankshaft at the top, in others at the bottom. If the choice is open, it is better to have the sparking plugs at the top to prevent oil and fuel draining into them when the engine is stationary.

There is usually one carburettor for each cylinder. Each must be connected to the crankcase via a valve to ensure the flow is one way — into the crankcase. There are two systems: the first makes use of the piston as a valve, while the second has a non-return valve of the reed type.

If the piston port system is used the carburettor is mounted on the lower part of the cylinder, whereas in the reed valve system the carburettor is mounted onto the crankcase.

Power and torque

For a cylinder of a certain size, the power output of an engine will increase as the rotational speed increases, the limit being determined by the strength of the components and the pumping and other losses associated with gases moving at very high speeds. Over the years speeds (revolutions per minute) have increased and continuous running at more than 6,000 rpm is now usual. To achieve a given horsepower for the least weight it is therefore desirable to have a small, high-speed engine.

Horse power is defined as the rate of doing work, one horse power being equal to 33,000 foot-pounds of work per minute. Thus the standard horse, lifting a weight by means of a rope and a pulley, should be able to walk at 330 ft/min when lifting a load of 100 lb.

In the case of an engine driving a rotating shaft, horse power

The CGS Hawk encloses the pilot in a dacron bag with transparent windows stretched around the tubular frame. The door panels on each side can be unzipped and removed completely.

Torque can be most easily visualised by considering an engine lifting a weight by means of a rope being wound round a drum.

If the drum is of one foot radius the torque will equal *weight on rope × 1 ft*. For each turn the drum will lift the weight 2π ft, so:

$$\text{Horse power} = \frac{2\pi \times \text{rpm} \times \text{torque}}{33,000} = \frac{\text{rpm} \times \text{torque}}{5,252}$$

from which we get:

$$\text{Torque} = \frac{5,252 \times \text{hp}}{\text{rpm}} \text{ lb–ft}$$

Example: If a 40 hp engine runs at 6,000 rpm, what is its torque?

$$\text{Torque} = \frac{5,252 \times 40}{6,000} = 35 \text{ lb–ft}$$

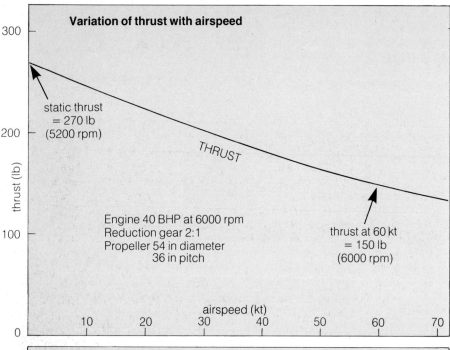

Variation of thrust with airspeed

static thrust
= 270 lb
(5200 rpm)

THRUST

Engine 40 BHP at 6000 rpm
Reduction gear 2:1
Propeller 54 in diameter
36 in pitch

thrust at 60 kt
= 150 lb
(6000 rpm)

thrust (lb)

airspeed (kt)

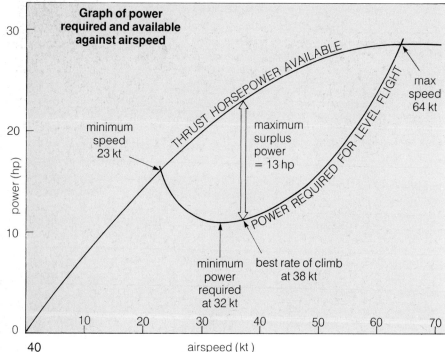

**Graph of power
required and available
against airspeed**

THRUST HORSEPOWER AVAILABLE

POWER REQUIRED FOR LEVEL FLIGHT

minimum
speed
23 kt

maximum
surplus
power
= 13 hp

max
speed
64 kt

minimum
power
required
at 32 kt

best rate of climb
at 38 kt

power (hp)

airspeed (kt)

determined by measuring the rpm of the engine and the torque being transmitted. (Torque = load × length of arm, and is measured in lb–ft.)

The graph of engine power at various speeds, using full throttle, is not a straight line, it curves off at high speed. Of the power which the engine produces, some is lost in driving auxiliaries, such as cooling fan and electric generator, some because of the resisting effect of the exhaust silencer and some in the reduction gear. Manufacturers' leaflets are seldom clear about the conditions under which the engine was tested, and claims may be optimistic.

Engine performance figures should relate to standard temperature and pressure conditions of 15°C and 1013.2mb. A higher temperature or a lower pressure will reduce the power output.

The propeller

The speed of an aeroplane in level flight and its rate of climb depend not on the horsepower of the engine, but on the thrust developed by the propeller, which is quite different. For a given horsepower the maximum thrust will be developed by a particular diameter of propeller rotating at a particular speed. The slower the

A Fuji Robin 2-cylinder engine in a Pathfinder. It produces 50 hp at 7000 rpm, 432 cc. Weight without reduction gear or exhaust 34kg. Note the inverted installation, reduction drive by 3 vee belts, twin carburettors with the fuel pump immediately above the right-hand one. The large circular casing on the left covers the cooling fan.

Twin engines on the Lazair. Two Rotax single-cylinder engines of 185 cc, 9.5 hp at 6000 rpm each. The 'biplane' propellers look improbable but work quite well. The engines are removed when de-rigging the aircraft. This is quick and simple.

The Pipistrelle with the König 3-cylinder radial built in West Germany. 430 cc and 30 hp at 4500 rpm. The weight without exhaust or reduction gear is 16 kg.

A Cayuna (USA) twin-cylinder engine on a Mirage. It is mounted in front of the wing and drives a propeller via a shaft running underneath the wing. 428 cc, 30 hp at 5500 rpm. Weight without reduction gear or exhaust 28 kg.

The Australian Skylark two-cylinder horizontally opposed simultaneous firing two-stroke. 320 cc, 24 hp at 5200 rpm. Weight without reduction gear or exhaust 14 kg. Here it is seen from above.

aircraft, the bigger the propeller should be, and the slower it should rotate.

The manpowered aircraft Gossamer Albatross, which flew across the English Channel in 1980, had an 'engine' of only about a quarter of one horsepower; the

Clearing a jammed reduction drive shaft. Do not work on your own engine unless you know what you are doing and have the proper tools.

pilot drove, by pedalling, a 13-ft diameter propeller at about 100 rpm.

Microlights are not so extreme, but to propel them with any degree of efficiency calls for a reduction gear to drive the propeller at about one half or one third of the engine speed. With the reduction gear fitted, the rpm will be reduced, the torque multiplied and the horse power will stay the same (assuming that the reduction gear efficiency is 100%). To use the example given above, with a reduction gear of 2:1 fitted, we obtain:

Component	Rpm	Torque	Horsepower
Engine	6,000	35 lb–ft	40
Propeller	3,000	70 lb–ft	40

It is undesirable to run a propeller with a top speed of more than about 75% of the speed of sound, because its efficiency is reduced and it starts to make a lot of noise. At sea level the speed of sound is about 660 knots (66,800 ft/min). 75% of this gives the following practical propeller diameters for various propeller rpm.

Propeller speed, rpm	2,000	4,000	6,000	8,000
Propeller diameter, ft	8	4	2.6	2

Once the propeller rpm and diameter are settled, the designer

can decide on the propeller pitch. The word 'pitch' is used in the same sense as when talking about a nut on a threaded bolt; it is the distance the nut advances along the bolt when it is turned through one revolution.

For various reasons, the pitch of a propeller is not constant from hub to tip. The pitch at three-quarters of the way out along the blade is taken as the reference and it is this which is stamped on the hub of a propeller. For example, '54 × 30' means a 54 inch diameter propeller of 30 inch pitch.

A propeller must of course be made to the correct 'hand'; putting a left-handed propeller on a right-handed engine merely pushes the aircraft backwards. If a correct propeller is put on back to front the effect is interesting; full rpm may be obtained and the thrust will act the right way, but it will not be as great as usual. A propeller is properly mounted when the slightly rounded edge is to the front (i.e. the direction in which the aeroplane will travel), and the sharper trailing edge to the rear.

The designer can select a propeller pitch which will allow the engine to develop its full rpm (and thus full power) at any airspeed he chooses. If he chooses a slow airspeed (fine pitch propeller), the aeroplane will take off and climb well, but in level flight the engine

These air filters may contain paper or felt inner filters. The paper ones do not last.

will overspeed unless it is throttled back. If he chooses a higher speed (coarse pitch propeller), the take off and climb will be poor, since the engine is being held back below its full power, although the top speed will be higher. On conventional aeroplanes, where the top speed may be five times the stalling speed, the problem of matching a propeller to the engine is impossible to solve satisfactorily; hence the variable pitch airscrew with fine pitch for take-off and coarser pitch for high-speed flying. On microlights with their smaller speed range the problem is less severe, but it does still exist.

Thrust

The static thrust is easily found by putting the aircraft on hard, smooth, level ground and using a spring balance on the tail to measure the thrust whilst the engine is running at full throttle.

In the air, the thrust cannot be measured directly without complicated instrumentation, but as the aircraft accelerates in level flight the following happens:

1 The airspeed increases.
  (This causes the propeller characteristics to change; less power is needed to achieve the

Fuji Robin showing reduction drive and fuel primer bulb. The air filters are made of foam.

same rpm, resulting in an increase of rpm.)

2 Because the rpm has increased, the engine develops more power.

3 Despite 2 and 3 above, the thrust produced by the propeller actually decreases.

The interplay of these factors is shown in the diagram on page 40.

Aircraft performance
If the thrust which the engine/propeller combination can develop at various airspeeds is known, it is possible to determine the thrust horsepower:

Thrust horsepower =
$$\frac{(\text{thrust, lb}) \times (\text{airspeed, ft/min})}{33,000}$$

It is also possible to calculate the drag of the aircraft at various speeds, and in the same way to work out the power needed to keep the aircraft flying level. These two curves are shown together on the illustration. The following should be noted:

1 The thrust horsepower at 0 airspeed is 0. This is correct — the horsepower is zero, although the actual thrust in pounds is at its maximum.

2 The power-required curve of the aircraft increases, as one would expect with increasing speed,

but down near the stall it also increases, due to the high induced drag.

3 The maximum speed in level flight is at the point where the two curves cross, and so is the minimum speed, right by the stall.

4 The maximum rate of climb is obtained at the speed at which there is the maximum surplus power, i.e. the vertical difference between the two curves. If, for example, this surplus power is 12 horsepower, and the aircraft weighs, all up, 660 lb, then the rate of climb will be given by:

Rate of climb =
$$\frac{(\text{surplus thrust horsepower}) \times 33,000}{\text{all-up weight}}$$
$$= \frac{13 \times 33,000}{660} \text{ ft/min} = 650 \text{ ft/min}$$

Unlike mechanical devices, such as chains and gears where the efficiency can be 95% or more, propellers are very inefficient; a small, high-revving one may be less than 40%, while a large, slow-speed one is no more than 70%. Thus the actual horsepower which the engine must develop is much higher than the thrust horsepower.

Engine reduction gears
Reductions are obtained by chain, gear, multiple V-belts, and by toothed belts as used on the

camshaft drives of many car engines. Problems have arisen in efforts to obtain a light, reliable reduction gear, but these are being overcome as the realisation dawns that there is no substitute for good engineering. Some engine makers are now selling engines with properly designed built-in reduction gearing.

Fuel consumption
There are fundamental laws which limit the amount of power that can be obtained by an internal combustion engine from a given quantity of fuel. Some engines are a little more efficient than others of the same class, but the variation is small. The relationship is best expressed as the number of horsepower hours which can be obtained from a unit volume of fuel (see table on p. 45).

The above figures give a reasonable estimate of the fuel consumption of an engine running fairly hard, but not at full throttle. At full throttle, or when running light, the consumption will be increased considerably (fewer hp-hours per gallon). Engines rated at 40 hp and operating comfortably at 30 hp output will use about 2 gal/hr if they are the four-stroke type and about 3 gal/hr if the two-stroke.

Fuel and mixture
Two-stroke engines are very

Type of engine	Horsepower hour per imperial gallon	Horsepower hour per US gallon	Horsepower hour per litre
Light diesel	19	16	4.2
Four-stroke petrol (Gasoline)	15	12.5	3.3
Two-stroke petrol (Gasoline)	10	8.3	2.2

sensitive to the types of fuel and oil supplied and mixture strength. The makers' instructions should be followed carefully and the mixing done accurately. If the engine is running too lean — with insufficient fuel — or with too rich a mixture, i.e. too much fuel in relation to the air, its performance will be affected. An expert can assess the mixture strength by examining the spark plugs immediately after a ground run and can then make carburettor adjustments as necessary, but do not experiment yourself.

The mixture in an engine which runs perfectly at ground level will gradually become richer as the aeroplane climbs, so to avoid rough running it is necessary to weaken the mixture. On most light aeroplanes there is a separate lever to do this, situated beside the throttle. Adjustment is made by bringing the mixture lever back progressively from the normal rich-

position as the aircraft gets above 5,000 feet or so. Few microlight engines are fitted with mixture controls.

Another problem arising when airborne which seldom occurs with ground-borne engines, is that of carburettor icing. The cooling which takes place within the carburettor as a result of air expanding in the choke tube leads to moisture freezing inside the carburettor. The critical factor is high humidity, rather than low temperature. The danger zone is when the air temperature is between 25°C and − 10°C with high humidity. Aeroplane engines usually have provision for providing hot air to the carburettor entry, and on some engines the carburettor body is heated. Microlight engines at present rarely have either provision.

Noise

Engine installation noise is due to:

1 The propeller, particularly its tip speed. Its proximity to parts of the aircraft or engine cowling can also have a considerable effect.

2 Exhaust noise. The greater the number of cylinders, the more even the noise, so it seems to become less obtrusive. The exhaust can be silenced effectively at the price of weight, cost and usually performance, although by tuning the exhaust for a particular engine speed the loss in performance may only be slight.

3 Mechanical noise. Bearings, gears, chains, tappets (on 4-strokes) — usually these are the least important.

4 Noise coming out of the carburettor inlets. This can be a large contributor since the inlet valve, whether piston skirts, reed valves on two-strokes, or poppet valves on four-strokes, is opening and closing several thousands of times per minute against a significant pressure differential. The solution is to fit a chamber of some volume upstream of the carburettor, as in the aircleaner of a motor car

engine. This reduces the
pulsations in the airflow through
the air entry.

5 The bell-like ringing of air
cooling fins and other parts.
Incidentally, a water-cooled
engine is.not quieter than an
air-cooled one because the
water 'damps' the noise; such an
engine runs more quietly without
any water at all! The reason is
that there are few fin-like parts to
vibrate.

If working on or close to the engine
disconnect the plug leads.

4. Instruments

Simple aeroplanes can be flown perfectly well without any instruments, and as a pilot you should practise not using them so that if they go wrong you will be able to fly without difficulty. Instruments are useful as aids to flying and navigating with precision, and the most important are:

Airspeed indicator (ASI)
Altimeter
Compass
Tachometer (rev counter)
Variometer — if you are interested in soaring and in what the air is doing.

Instruments normally fitted on microlights may not provide accurate information either because they were never designed for aviation use (e.g. wrist altimeter), or because the airflow

Halfway across the English Channel with not much except the instruments to look at. A typical panel in a trike — the most prominent instrument being the variometer. The pilot has not taken his feet off the rudder pedals; the bar near his feet is the nose wheel steering for use on the ground. Control is by weightshift.

A streamlined panel holding an ASI and altimeter, originally designed for hang gliders. On this microlight it is wire-braced to prevent vibration.

past them causes errors. This is particularly true of the *airspeed indicator*.

Airspeed indicator

The ASI works on the difference in pressure caused by the speed of the aircraft through the air and the static pressure of the atmosphere. The pressure caused by the aircraft's speed is obtained by a pitot head (pressure) or a venturi (suction), and the static pressure by sensing holes on the outside of the pitot or venturi. In each case the pressure, or suction, is transmitted by small tubes to the airspeed instrument, which is a sensitive differential pressure gauge.

On some installations there is no proper sensing head for the static; it is just a hole in the instrument. Its accuracy is now dependent on its location and large errors will result, particularly at high speeds, if it is mounted in a zone of positive or negative pressure. The ASI can only give accurate readings if the sensing heads are placed in clear air well away from the wing and fuselage.

If you install your own ASI find out from the manufacturers the best position for the venturi or pitot head. They should know this from the aircraft's test flight programme.

As you gain height into less dense air your aircraft will be flying faster than shown on the

The Winter Airspeed Indicator, which senses air pressure in a venturi. It is an accurate instrument but its accuracy is useless if the venturi is mounted in any position on the aircraft where the static pressure of the atmosphere is altered by the airflow over the structure or the wing.

A wrist altimeter. The velcro strap can also be used to attach it to the tubular structure.

instrument. This should not interfere with your navigation calculations unless you wish to fly high in freezing air. It also does not affect the *indicated* speed at which the aircraft stalls, although the true stall speed does increase as you go higher. What the instrument actually reads is the indicated airspeed (IAS), and when it is corrected for errors in the instrument and its location (pressure error) the speed is termed the equivalent airspeed (EAS).

Altimeter

This is also a pressure-controlled instrument. It is actually a barometer translating the air pressure into feet or metres on an instrument dial or digital readout. It will be affected by pressure changes caused by depressions and anticyclones. Altimeters, in fact, rarely show the true height of the aircraft. If you set your altimeter to sea level before take-off it will show you your height above the sea but not above the ground. If you set it at airfield height at take-off it will show you your height above the airfield — which may be useful for circuit practice, but not very useful for a cross-country flight.

However you have set your altimeter on the ground it continues to be affected by the constantly changing air pressure. If you are flying towards an approaching depression your altimeter will increasingly show you height that you have not got. This could be dangerous if you are flying over hilly country in poor visibility or low cloud. In anticyclonic conditions your altimeter will show a little less height than you actually have, which is usually no problem.

If your altimeter has a millibar scale you can set it accurately for the prevailing pressure by asking the local flying club or air traffic controller for a QNH (altitude above sea level based on the local pressure), or QFE (altitude above the ground based on the local pressure). More important for you, flying a microlight, is that you do not fly in the sort of bad weather which makes this degree of accuracy important, and that if you do, you understand how your altimeter is being affected.

Compass

The most important attributes of any compass you are going to use in the air are:

a that it settles quickly on to a new heading

b it is easy to read — without any chance of it being read 180° the wrong way!

Some pilots like to make up their own more sophisticated panels. This has a digital altimeter and includes airspeed indicator and variometer.

Using the compass is dealt with in Chapter 11.

Tachometer

This tells you the speed in revolutions per minute (rpm) at

The Triflier's nose dome is shaped so that instruments can be fitted just above the zip-up cockpit. They are, left to right, altimeter, variometer, and a combined cylinder head and exhaust gas temperature gauge. ▶

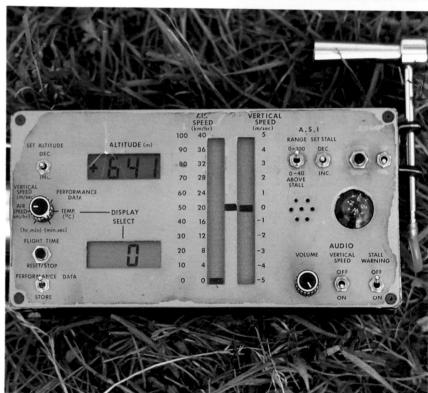

50

which your engine is running; and it is very useful in determining power for the most economical cruise, or maximum cruise speed.

You should learn what revs your engine will give at full throttle on the

The panel of the side-by-side Duet. The flight instruments are on the left, where the first pilot sits, with engine instruments on the right. The hanging knob operates the wheel brake.

ground when it is in good condition. If you find subsequently that you cannot obtain these revs on run-up before take-off you will know that your engine is not developing full power. Find out why before you fly. There will be a very slight difference in maximum power when the weather is very hot or very cold.

On microlight engines tachometers are electrically operated.

Variometer

The 'vario' is an essential instrument for glider pilots, and interesting for any pilot who wants to know what the air in which he is flying is doing. On a weather-sensitive microlight it is particularly helpful.

The variometer indicates the actual speed at which the aircraft is rising — gaining height, or sinking — losing height. On a glider this indication is the actual speed at which the air is rising less the rate at which the glider is descending through the air, e.g. if the thermal is rising at 5 knots and the glider's sink rate is 3 knots the variometer will show 2 knots up. If you are flying level under power and your variometer shows 2 knots up you are in air rising at 2 knots — unless,

A simple panel with airspeed indicator, altimeter, and ignition key.

51

A windspeed indicator is often used as a simple guide to airspeed. The air pressure entering it at the bottom lifts a plate which indicates airspeed on the scale. It is an aid, not an accurate instrument.

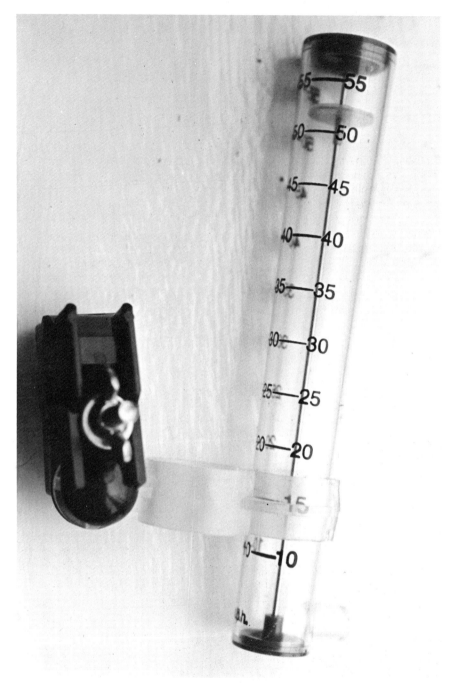

of course, you are not actually flying level!

The principle on which a variometer works is that the instrument is positioned between free air and air contained in a capacity (vacuum flask). As the aircraft rises into air of lower pressure air flows out from the capacity, through the instrument (which is caused to register) and into the open air. When the aircraft descends the air pressure inside the capacity becomes less than the air outside, so air flows through the instrument into the flask.

Some variometers are operated electrically.

Variometer. If the right-hand (green) pellet rises in its tube the aircraft is gaining height. If the left-hand (red) pellet rises it is losing height.

5. Pre-flight checks

The best way to ensure that nothing will go wrong with your aircraft in the air is to check it properly before take off: try pushing your microlight along when you are 1,000 feet up and out of petrol! There are three separate pre-flight checks:

a Rigging check

b Daily inspection (preflight)
c Pre-take off check

Rigging check

This should be carried out completely every time you assemble your aircraft, even if it has only been partly dismantled to facilitate some minor repair. Because microlights come in so many shapes and sizes there can be no set system, so you should work out a logical one for your own

The little Microbipe with a span of 5.48 m (18 ft) and an empty weight of 74.8 kg (165 lb). However good it looks you should always stand back and look at any aircraft you are inspecting for symmetry and completeness.

Any tailskid is easily damaged by heavy landings or rough ground. Excessive loads on it could bed the stern post or jam the rudder hinge. Always inspect carefully.

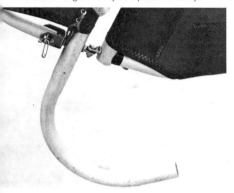

Inspect ends of cables. Thimbles should no be distorted and plastic sheathing must stop short of the talurit swage.

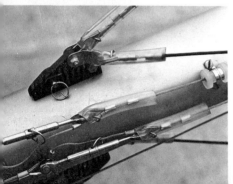

Check that turnbuckles are in safety. Here thread is exposed on two of them. If turnbuckles are close together check they are unable to interfere with each other.

aircraft to ensure that every part will be checked. Many pilots start at the nose of the microlight, work around one wing, check the tail, work around the second wing, return to the nose and finally check cockpit and engine. The question to ask yourself every time is 'Have I put it together properly?'

1 When the aircraft is first assembled stand back and look at it as a whole. It should look symmetrical; the wings should have the same amount of dihedral and the tailplane or canard should be parallel to a mean line through the wings. If it is not you must find out why. Check that no end fitting of any of the bracing wires is kinked over at the thimble. Check that any distortion in the wing-covering fabric is the same on both sides. If there are ripples on only one side look inside for damage or incorrect assembly.

2 Go now to the nose and to the centre section attachment of the wings. Are the wings correctly attached at the front spar or tube? Are bolts fully home so that flight loads are taken on the bolt shank and not on the thread of the bolt? Are bolts properly retained in

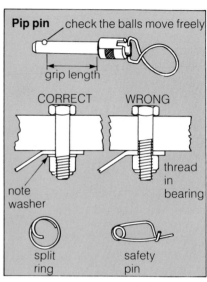

Pip pin check the balls move freely

grip length

CORRECT WRONG

note washer

thread in bearing

split ring

safety pin

position by lock nuts (which cannot be moved by strong fingers) or by split or safety pins? If a pip pin is used are the spring-loaded balls visible and extended? Could the pip pin handle be inadvertently pulled by a control cable fitting?

3 Move out along the leading edge of the wing. Check that any bracing wires on both the top and the wing (for landing loads) and underneath the wing (for flying loads) are properly attached at both wing and centre section ends. Look for kinked thimbles, security of talurit (nicopress) attachments at cable ends, and make sure that all cables are properly tensioned. If one cable is slacker or tighter than expected FIND OUT WHY. Open

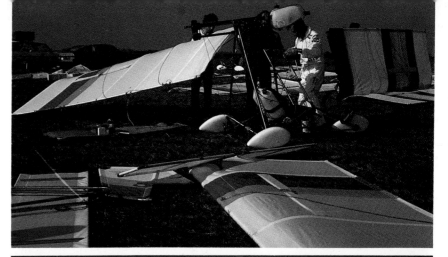

wing inspection panels to check any connections or control pulleys inside, then replace them. Go round the wing to the ailerons. Check that moving the surface moves both the aileron on the other wing and the control column (stick). Check the trailing edge and any battens for damage and security.

4 Check the fuselage and the wing's rear spar fittings. Are they properly attached? Are any control cables and pulleys to the tail controls moving freely? If you have a trike with a floating cross tube check that this is free.

5 Check the tail is properly attached to the tailboom or fuselage, that bracing wires are properly connected and tensioned, and that rudder and elevator control surfaces move fully, freely, and IN THE CORRECT SENSE. More than one accident has been caused by a pilot taking off with his elevators connected the wrong way round. If there are no control surface stops check that movement of one control surface is not causing interference with another.

When rigging aircraft, particularly if you are in a hurry, it is easy to forget something.

Rigging a Pathfinder starts with unloading the bags from the car roof rack.

The wing is nearly ready. The next bag contains the tail unit.

The Lazair engines are removed each time the aircraft is de-rigged. If they are not properly attached and checked they could shake themselves off in the air.

Daily inspection (often known as 'The Preflight')

Although this implies just one inspection on the day prior to flying you should also thoroughly inspect the aircraft following any heavy landing, if it seems to be handling differently in the air, or whenever it has been left unattended in a public place; a spectator may have tripped over the tailplane and departed unaware that he could have caused serious damage, or you could be the victim of some thoughtless souvenir hunter.

Use the same 'walk round' inspection procedure as for the rigging check, starting at the nose. Now you should also check for damage and wear and tear as well as security of fittings. Look at the undercarriage. Are the tyres correctly inflated? Are suspension rubbers in good condition? If there is a wheel brake, does it work?

Along the wing you are looking for damage to the fabric covering and for broken stitches; also for denting or distortion of aluminium tubing. Look carefully at the wing tip in case it has received damage from being scraped along the ground.

Move round to the fuselage tubing. If there are three or four small-diameter tubes they must all

6 Repeat procedure for the other wing, finishing at the nose.
7 Go to the cockpit and check again that the stick and rudder pedals are moving the control surfaces in the correct sense, e.g. when the stick is moved back the elevator surface on the tail goes up. Check that any removable instruments or fairings are present and correctly attached.
8 Now it is the turn of the engine. This only becomes part of the

rigging check if it, its propeller, or the fuel tank are removed when the aircraft is derigged. On the Lazair, which has two engines, this is the case. Both should be checked for security of attachment and that fuel lines are not trapped. If the propeller has been removed the nuts should be locked on to the bolts. Finally, items such as fuel tanks and batteries must be installed. The rigging check is not finished until the aircraft is complete.

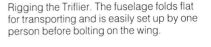

Rigging the Triflier. The fuselage folds flat for transporting and is easily set up by one person before bolting on the wing.

be checked, particularly if one appears to be slightly bowed or bent. The tail — or the canard — is usually of light construction and is easily damaged, even when in a hangar. It should receive special attention, particularly if landings have been on rough ground.

Aluminium tube aircraft are not ideally suited to continuous vibration over long periods such as microlights may have to withstand. Bolt holes tend to become enlarged or elongated, especially near the source of the vibration (the engine), and on the tail. This should be watched for on *every* inspection.

The cockpit should now be looked at for seat security including the harness, which should also be checked for fraying. Controls should be rechecked to make sure that any instruments are working. Remember that most airspeed indicators are pressure-sensitive instruments using a pitot head or venturi for their operation. If your ASI does not work do not attempt to make it do so by blowing, as a strong blast of human breath will probably ruin it for ever.

If your cockpit has fairings any panels must be properly fastened. Even a small panel coming adrift in flight could fly into the propeller and, if this is shattered in flight, further damage to the structure is

If the undercarriage uses rubber shock cords, check that the rubber is not perishing and is still doing the job for which it was intended.

Are the propeller nuts fully home and are they secure? Nuts should be locked with wire, split pins, safety pins, or split rings so that they cannot loosen.

Is the fuel tank secure, the filler cap on properly, and the vent unblocked? Do you have enough fuel?

◄ The cockpit is important. Is the harness attached correctly or is it frayed? Is the seat cushion attached properly? Is the wind-meter being used as an airspeed indicator properly positioned and secure?

What can go wrong? The drive shaft has ► become bent, partly due to the vee belts being too tight: as a result, in flight, the propeller was just touching the exhaust pipe near the bottom of the picture. This had worn it away to a depth of almost one centimetre, so the propeller had to be discarded.

by no means impossible.

The engine should be inspected for security of its attachment to the aircraft. Look carefully for cracks around the bolt holes and for the condition and tension of the reduction drive vee or toothed belts. Check that the exhaust pipe and silencer are not showing signs of splitting or coming adrift.

Propellers are easily damaged by stones thrown up on take-off and so the blades should be looked at for dents and splits. Finally, the aircraft's tank should be filled with the correct petrol/oil mixture. There should be a good margin for the proposed flight; about 40 per cent over calculated flight time is about right. Make sure the tank vent is open and check that there is no water in the fuel tank.

If you are interrupted while doing your daily inspection you should either begin again at the beginning or continue the inspection with a repeat of the last item you checked, so as to avoid any chance of leaving something out. It is no bad thing to give your aircraft its own log book, and to note

On this aircraft the tailplane is not parallel to the wing. It may be strong enough but it neither improves the flying characteristics or looks right. Maybe a previous owner did a bad repair.

rigging checks, daily inspections, and any repairs and replacements. If nothing else it will make the aircraft easier to sell when you want to buy your next dream ship.

Pre-take-off check

This is only a brief and simple check, but you should do it before EVERY take off so that it becomes a deeply ingrained habit.

To help your memory there is a mnemonic: **CHIFTA.**

C   CONTROLS   Full and free movement (a stone could have wedged in the elevator hinge when you taxied in). Control surfaces moving in the correct sense. Any spoilers closed. Any brakes off.

H   HARNESS   Properly fastened. Helmet on and correctly fastened.

I   INSTRUMENTS   All present and connected up; altimeter set. Batteries on.

F   FUEL   Tank full of correct mixture; cap secure; vent open. Fuel switched on.

T   TRIM   (If any) set for take off. Cockpit load within permitted limits or necessary ballast.

A   ALL CLEAR   Ahead, above, and behind. Ready to go.

Depending on local circumstances the engine may or may not be running when you do this check. If it is you are ready to move to the take-off point. If you decide to postpone take-off and get out of the aircraft, you should repeat your checks before the new start.

Inspecting your aircraft

Rigging check

Every time you assemble your microlight to check that it has been correctly put together and is complete.

Pre-flight inspection

Every day before you start flying, after every heavy landing, and whenever your aircraft has been left unattended in a public place. You should look for damage and wear and tear.

Take-off check

Before every take-off so that nothing is forgotten:
C CONTROLS Full and free movement, spoilers closed
H HARNESS Properly fastened and helmet on
I INSTRUMENTS Connected, batteries on, altimeter set
F FUEL Tank full, cap secure, vent open, fuel on
T TRIM (If any) set for take off, cockpit load correct
A ALL CLEAR Ahead, above, and behind

6. Maintenance and repair

Looking after an aircraft has to be done thoroughly since the penalty for careless work or simple mistakes can be great. Every part of the structure is necessary, so the whole aircraft is either serviceable or unserviceable. If you allow yourself on to the slippery slope of thinking 'this will be all right for a day or so' your flying will be less safe.

Apart from rigging and pre-flight inspections (Chapter 5) you should give your aircraft more thorough periodic inspections. These will almost certainly be called for by the manufacturer and listed in the owner's manual which should come with the aircraft. The schedule usually covers:

a minor inspections, which should be done after a given number of flying hours, and

b major inspections, after a larger number of hours, or once a year.

Nosewheel and rudder pedal assembly. This is an area which takes the kicks – and a great deal of wear. It is strongly built in the first place but needs just as careful maintenance as the wing. Note the plate between the rudder pedals which is linked to the wheel fork and by cable to the rudder itself. This ensures that when taxiing the nose wheel turns in the same sense as the rudder – right foot, right rudder, right turn.

Since there is often little inclination in the summer months to stop flying and overhaul your aircraft, it is sensible that a thorough maintenance job is done in the winter. If you are not sure how far you should strip down the aircraft, contact the manufacturer for advice. Keep a record of all inspections, work done, parts replaced, etc., including the name of the person who did the work.

If you are going to do the work yourself you will soon find that you are in a sort of 'Jekyll and Hyde' situation. You are the inspector — to decide what is not serviceable. Then you become the repairer — to decide *why* the unserviceability has occurred and *how* to put it right. Finally, you again become the inspector — to decide if the aircraft is now serviceable.

Maintenance work can be divided into 3 categories:
a adjustment;
b replacement, and
c repair.

Adjustment
This includes tyre pressure, control cable tightness, and carburettor and ignition adjustments. Whenever possible proper equipment, such as a cable tensioning device, should be used; the eye rarely gives an accurate enough answer.

Replacement and repair
Having discovered something unserviceable it is most important to find out why the defect has occurred. Is it just wear and tear, or has the component been overloaded — either when rigging or in flight? You need to know :
a the importance of the component in a structural or control sense, and
b whether the full extent of the defect or damage has been discovered.

For example, apparent slight landing damage at the wingtip may well have resulted in damage to the wing root fittings on both the wing *and* the fuselage. Such damage may not only consist of bent fittings, bolts or tubes, but also of

If your engine stops – maybe you ran out of fuel – and you land in water you will have a big maintenance and repair job, even if the water is fresh. The salty sea would be worse. You have to check the aircraft all over for distortion and damage; some of this will occur in rescuing the aircraft. If you land in the sea, hose the aircraft and engine down with fresh water as soon as possible and then inspect it very carefully.

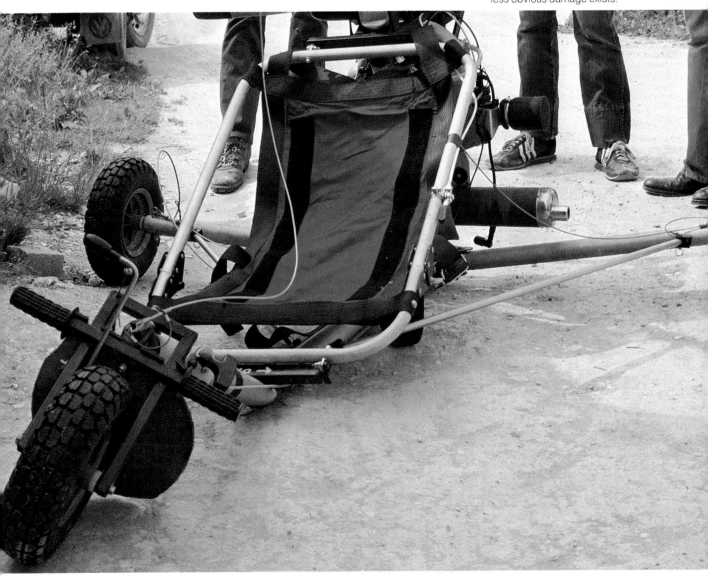

Typical heavy landing damage. The main axle is bent and the nose wheel assembly looks sad. You should always carefully inspect the rest of the aircraft in case some less obvious damage exists.

small cracks in the fittings themselves. As a minimum requirement, these should be looked for with a good magnifying glass.

Having determined the full extent of the problem the decision has to be taken as to whether a repair can be made, e.g. straightening a slightly bowed tube, or whether the item(s) need to be replaced. The difficulty is usually in deciding how far it is safe to go by repairing.

Tubes

The three most likely sources of trouble are :

a dents or bends,

b elongated bolt holes, and

c corrosion, particularly from sea water or sea air.

If any of these is more than very slight, or if the tube has been previously straightened, it should be replaced. In some cases wear in a bolt hole can be repaired by reaming out the existing hole and fitting an oversize bolt, but since almost all the tubes carry large structural loads expert advice should be obtained.

Cables

Examine for :

a wear and damage at the point where the cable is joined back on itself, and

b damage to the cable stranding. Look at the thimble at the end of

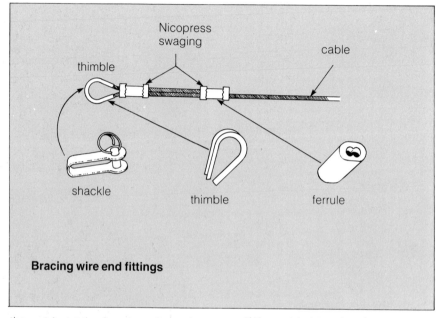

Bracing wire end fittings

the cable, at the ferrules where the cable is swaged, and then at the cable itself.

Two sorts of cable may be used: galvanised, and stainless steel. Ferrules used on galvanised cable are made of aluminium while those on stainless steel are of copper, sometimes cadmium plated. Ferrules of the wrong material lead to rapid corrosion.

Some cables have a plastic coating, and it is essential to remove this from the parts of the cable to be joined. Fitting ferrules on top of the plastic risks the cable being pulled out.

If the cable is, or has been, kinked or bent examine it carefully by gently untwisting or bending it the other way to see if any tiny wires stick out. A cable which has been working around a small pulley may have broken wires which cannot be found except by this test, or by examination with a magnifying glass.

Corrosion

Corrosion can occur on any metal fitting. If it is appreciable, particularly on a highly stressed part, there is no alternative to replacement. Corrosion can be

reduced by :
a keeping the aircraft in a dry, ventilated place (not in a wet bag);
b lubricating parts which have to be left bare, such as hinge pins or rigging bolts;
c hosing down the aircraft with

fresh water after flying near the sea or landing on sand.

Fabric
Damage includes :
a chafing or nipping between metal parts,
b frayed and broken stitching,

c weakening caused by exposure to ultraviolet light (usually due to the aircraft being parked outside for days at a time).

If you have any doubts about the strength of the fabric have it tested by the manufacturer or a good sailmaker.

Seat harnesses are made of fabric so the above applies, although the most likely source of damage is where the straps bear on seat edges or metal fittings.

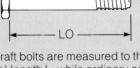

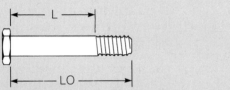

Aircraft bolts are measured to the plain (grip) length L, while ordinary commercial bolts are measured to the total length of the shank LO.

Wing nut: the hole is for locking wire

1 Ordinary nut.   2 Thin nut, used as a lock nut on turnbuckles.
3 Slotted nut.   4 Castellated nut.   5 Stiff nut, with nylon or composition insert inside head.   6 Stiff nut with thin parallel cuts in head.

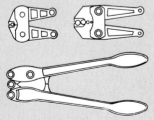

Nicopress swaging tool

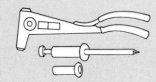

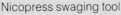

Pop rivetting tool

Locking
All bolts and nuts on aircraft must be properly locked by :
a stiff nuts,
b split pins, through slotted or castellated nuts, or
c locking wire through slotted or castellated nuts, where a number of bolts are close together (as on a propeller boss).

The purpose of locking a nut is to prevent it loosening. The practice of putting a split ring through a hole near the end of the bolt is not satisfactory since the nut can work loose before being stopped by the ring.

Where there are pins through control fittings a split pin should be used. A safety pin or strong split ring should be used only if the fitting is frequently disconnected as part of de-rigging or assembling the aircraft.

Any turnbuckles must be checked for locking and also for being 'in safety'. This means that there is enough thread engaged within the barrel. The turnbuckle barrel should either show no thread exposed at the end, or have little holes through which you can poke a wire to see if enough thread has been engaged.

General safety
Locking wire and split pins should *never* be re-used, but thrown away. Stiff nuts must be stiff to turn. If they turn easily throw them away.

If possible always put in bolts, pins, and pip pins with the head at the top or in front, so that gravity and wind will keep them in. If the head is at the bottom and the nut vibrates loose the bolt could just drop out.

Bolts, nuts and threads
There is a bewildering variety of threads in use, and it is essential not to put on a nut which does not fit or screw the wrong bolt into a tapped hole in an expensive engine casting. There is also a considerable range of threads in use on pipe fittings, such as fuel pipes, valves, etc. Bolts should be of a quality suitable for aircraft.

66

Spanners
AF means 'across flats'. This refers to the width across the flats of the bolt which the spanner fits.

Looking after the engine

The reliability of any engine, particularly a two-stroke, depends on the conscientiousness with which it is maintained.

Fuel
Most problems are likely to stem from using the wrong fuel/oil mix or from dirty or polluted fuel. The fuel must be the correct grade and it must be mixed with the oil specified by the manufacturer in the right proportions. This cannot be done accurately enough by using only the marks on the container in which it comes. It is worth buying a proper measuring cylinder from a photographic shop and doing it precisely.

The container in which you mix the fuel must obviously be clean, and if the weather is cold the fuel and oil must be well mixed by shaking before you pour them into the aircraft fuel tank. If you use the wrong mix you risk :
a overheating or seizing the engine, and
b oiling up the spark plugs.

There is evidence that fuel/oil mixes deteriorate with keeping. If the tank has held fuel over the winter without the aircraft being flown, it is sensible to discard this fuel and start your flying in the spring with a new, clean mix.

Filters
There should be a coarse filter at the exit from the tank and a fine filter nearer the carburettor. These must be cleaned or replaced regularly. It may seen obvious but unless a fuel tank has a vent to let air in, fuel cannot get to the engine and so it will stop. Ensure that the vent does not become blocked with greasy dust. One aviator flying across the USA had 72 forced landings before someone told him what the trouble was!

Spares
To maintain a fuel system properly you will need a supply of the correct clips, pipes, washers, gaskets for carburettor and fuel pump, and various other spares. Get them from the manufacturer when you buy the engine.

Carburettor
Carburettors are complicated so do not experiment without expert advice — unless you are absolutely sure you know what you are doing.

Ignition

Two-stroke engines are sensitive to the type of spark plug and the ignition timing. Plugs must be kept clean and replaced at regular intervals. When checking spark plug gaps it is easy to get confused with inch and metric feeler gauges. Inch gauges are normally marked in thousandths of an inch (20 means 0.020″ or 20 thou). Metric feelers can be marked with or without a decimal point in hundredths of one millimetre (either .50 or 50 means 0.5 mm — which equals 20 thou).

Adjustments to the ignition system cannot be done properly without electrical timing gear.

The maintenance of the rest of the engine is really a matter of keeping it clean and free from corrosion — and hayseeds in between the air cooling fins — and ensuring that it remains properly bolted to its mountings. This also applies to the exhaust pipe and silencer which will soon work loose if they are allowed to.

If you think you are not getting the power that you should, ask to borrow a compression tester from your local garage. This will show you the compression you are actually getting when you screw it in to a spark plug socket and turn the engine over.

Propeller

Small nicks and bruises in a wooden propeller can be sanded out, filled, or covered with a metal sheath on each leading edge — provided you do not end up with an unbalanced airscrew. If the propeller is split, or any damage is more than 2 mm deep, it should be returned to the manufacturer for repairs, or thrown away.

When you replace a propeller check that :

a it is on the right way round
b it is on square and rotates true
c that the nuts are all done up properly and are wired securely.

Whenever you work on the propeller when it is attached to the engine REMOVE THE PLUG LEADS, in case the electrical system fails live or the switch is knocked onto 'contact' inadvertently.

Finally, as with the airframe, keep a log of all work done.

Do–it–yourself kits

Many microlights can be bought in kit form, which is a good way of getting to know your aircraft and to save money. But building an aircraft has to be more than a good idea if you want to end up with a complete microlight; more than half the kits bought never take the air,

simply because the work is never finished.

If you are serious about building from a kit you need a workshop or clean, empty garage long enough to hold half the wing (about 6 m or 20 ft), and high enough to rig the fuselage and tail, or at least the tail. Unless you want to work only by daylight and in summer your workshop will need good lighting and some heating. The amount of warmth will depend on whether you want to work clumsily with cold fingers, and on the demands of any glues or resins. Some (e.g. epoxy, polyester, aerolite, etc.) do not cure quickly or properly unless the temperature is over 15°C (59°F).

You also need tools and the ability to use them. These will vary according to the type of construction, different techniques being required for a wood microlight than for one made of aluminium tubes. In addition you need a strong, rigid workbench with a substantial vice. If it is a metalworker's vice fit it with hardwood facing strips so that aluminium tubes and fittings cannot be scratched or bruised.

How long to build?

If your 'workshop' is to be your living room there are likely to be members of the family who will demand to know how long you are going to clutter the place up. It will

If you think of building from a kit make sure you buy a good one. This kit provides sets of plastic-covered cards containing all the nuts, bolts, and fittings for each part of the aircraft.

be longer than you think, so do not make rash promises. Most kit manufacturers give an estimated number of hours it will take to construct the microlight. This is usually optimistic, and in any case must be realistically divided into the working periods you have available. If, for example, the brochure says 20 hours, double it. If you now plan for five evenings of 4 hours plus two weekend days of

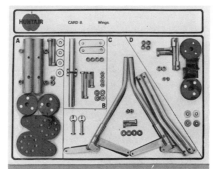

One of 10 cards supplied covered in shrunk plastic which come with the Pathfinder kit.

The second of two wing cards and the ▶ instruction book.

Some pilots fit foam or plastic streamline sleeves on the structural tubes to reduce drag. Could they come off in flight and hit the propeller? This pilot has painted his propeller so that it will be really conspicuous.

Working on a new aircraft or repairing an older one. Use the only correct replacement nuts, bolts, or fittings. This plastic covered card was supplied by the manufacturer. ▶

10 hours each (you are enthusiastic at this stage) this gives a total period of one full week; doubled, it is 2 weeks. You will find that your good intentions about hard work are eroded by having to answer the telephone, talk to friends who come to see how you are getting on, plus going to the shops to replace your broken hacksaw blades. Before you realise it you are almost through the second week. If you are constructing a wood or glass fibre microlight you could easily take a year. By this time enthusiasm could be waning and other pressures on the increase. This is why, to succeed, you need a good workshop that you do not have to use for anything else.

Which kit to buy?

The simplest microlight to build is one of wire braced and tube construction; however, your own choice will be affected by what you want as the end result — the flying machine. For example, will it have the performance and handling to satisfy you as a pilot? It is not sensible to buy an excellent kit if the performance of the aircraft is so low that you will be bored flying it after a few hours.

You will need to check the following before buying:

a   Does the aircraft type meet any national airworthiness

b How have other builders of this type of aircraft fared?

c Is the kit provided with a detailed, complete, and clear set of drawings and instructions, and an owner's handbook?

d Are all tubes already drilled?

e Are all nuts and bolts for each component or area of construction separately packaged and marked?

f Are all cables cut to length and requirements? swaged — or is there just a big coil of wire that you have to measure and cut yourself?

g Does the kit include 'fixture' items, such as seat cushions and pilot's harness, and instruments?

h Does the engine package include an owner's handbook and special tools?

i Can you buy the kit a part at a time, e.g., can you buy the wings now and the fuselage in three months' time?

j Can you *easily* buy a replacement for some item, such as a tube or bracket that you have damaged or lost?

k Are you supplied with a list of special tools or equipment (such as a nicopress swager) which you will have to buy in addition — or are they supplied as part of the kit?

l Does the manufacturer offer to inspect your finished aircraft, if brought to the factory, free of charge or for a set fee?

If the kit is deficient in any of these items and the manufacturer is not able to give you a reasonable explanation, or there is no owner's handbook available, do not be persuaded into making a purchase. There are excellent kits available, but a few are not good buys — usually because too much is left for you to do, things which should have been done at the factory to achieve the necessary accuracy. It is in your own interests

The tools you need to build a Tiger Cub from a kit

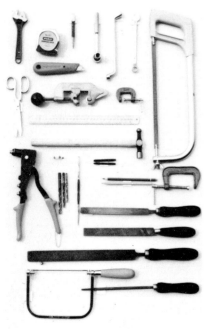

Bolts, nuts and threads

UNF   Stands for *unified fine*. This type of thread was introduced in the UK, USA and Canada to help ensure compatibility of parts in the three countries. It replaces the BSF (British Standard Fine) and USS (United States Standard). It is the most common non-metric thread used on aircraft.

Metric   The ISO (International Organisation for Standardisation) 'M' series of metric threads is now used extensively in Japan and many parts of Europe. (In the UK the number of these threads is on the increase, but in the USA there is much less demand for them.)

BA   The British Association thread is still used on some electrical equipment and, in the 2, 4, and 6 BA sizes, on several aircraft fittings. It is actually a metric thread, using rather odd dimensions.

Whitworth   These are coarse thread bolts used on agricultural machinery and, in large sizes, in the construction industry. They and their metric equivalent are not used on aircraft.

BSP   The British Standard Pipe is still the universal pipe thread. The 1/8″ and 1/4″ BSP sizes are sometimes used on fuel pipe fittings. The sizes refer to the bore of a nominal pipe, so the 1/8″ BSP thread is actually 0.382″ diameter.

to have the aircraft inspected at regular intervals during construction by a qualified engineer; he cannot be expected to examine and approve your beautifully finished product in its final stage if he cannot see its internal construction without having to cut holes in it.

If you buy a kit and complete it properly you have every right to

feel satisfied, but do not then rush into the air without further thought:

a   Is your experience as a pilot sufficient to fly the aircraft without additional instruction?

b   How long is it since you last flew — many builders concentrate so hard on completing their 'dream ship' that they do not realise they are seriously out of practice

technical agent, or a qualified microlight engineer or inspector.

Do not fly your aircraft until any necessary repairs or replacements have been carried out.

The Tiger Cub comes in kit form. The total of 7 kit packs can be bought one at a time so you do not have to find all the money at once.

c Have you test flown anything — even tried to write a handling report about a bicycle?

d If you test fly your microlight do you know what you are looking for as regards speeds and handling characteristics etc.?

Unless you really do have a great deal of experience ask a competent test pilot to do the first few flights. And before he — or

anyone — flies it have it thoroughly inspected by a qualified engineer (or the manufacturer). If it has to have an airworthiness document and insurance, see that it does.

Secondhand aircraft

If you are looking for a secondhand aircraft, before you buy :

a find out if it has been crashed or damaged and what repairs were done; if it does not have a log book your suspicions should be alerted;

b have it thoroughly checked over by the manufacturer, his

7. Safety on the ground

As microlights are often operated from fields where people, including children, may be wandering about, the pilot has a responsibility to avoid causing injury. Propellers are the most likely source of damage so you need to operate with considerable discipline. Never work on your aircraft while the propeller is turning. Stop it before you get out of the seat and check that the ignition is switched off. Unfortunately this is not always completely effective on two-strokes and so the engine should always be treated as if it were live. If you need to run the engine to check, for example, suspected propeller vibration make foolproof arrangements to keep people clear.

Each time, before you start your engine, look all around for children or dogs, call loudly 'starting engine' and when all clear start up. If possible ask another pilot to help prevent people from coming too close to you.

Engine starting

Propellers can be swung by hand, but with very light propellers and high revving engines a recoil or electric starter is much safer. Whatever is available it is obviously sensible to use a set procedure for engine starting, so that anyone involved will know whether the engine is live or not — be it on a big aeroplane or a microlight. If you have a helper follow this routine:

1 Helper calls, 'Fuel on, switch(es) off'.
2 Pilot checks and repeats, 'Fuel on, switch(es) off', and primes engine if needed.
3 Pilot calls, 'Ready to start'.
4 Helper calls, 'Throttle set, contact'.
5 Pilot repeats, 'Throttle set, contact', and switches on the ignition.
6 Helper swings the propeller or pulls the recoil cord. If the engine does not start helper calls, 'switch(es) off'.
7 Pilot switches off and calls, 'switch(es) off'.

When the helper is ready to restart he goes over the procedure again.

Before leaving the aircraft the pilot is responsible for switching off the ignition and, if need be, switching off the fuel.

Fuel and fire

Where combustible fuel is present there is always a fire risk. Never leave your fuel containers lying around in long grass or in places where they can be driven over. If

Avoid starting the engine on your own if possible. If the throttle were to be left open by mistake the aircraft could jerk forward, knocking over the pilot.

This is more sensible. The helper is not only doing the work but is in a better position to keep people clear of the propeller.

Hand swinging a lightweight propeller on a high revving engine is not ideal. If you do it do not stand on slippery ground or wear flapping coats or scarves.

Before starting the engine check that people are clear. Small children cannot be expected to know the danger, and may move quickly into it.

— and as it starts move clear.

Engines can be started using a battery driven 'screwdriver' fitting into a socket in the propeller boss. Early RAF aircraft used a Hucks starter which worked in this way.

When refuelling check that the correct petrol/oil mixture or fuel is being put in, that there is an adequate filter, and that you are putting in enough.

or mix of fuel. Keep a fire extinguisher handy, and if you smoke set a good example by not doing so when you are handling fuel.

Parachutes

Parachutes are intended to save your life but may only do so if they are properly looked after. Ordinary personal parachutes should not be left in the sun or among oily tools, or allowed to get wet. They should be repacked regularly according to the maker's instructions. Many of the more recent parachutes produced for hang gliders and microlights are of the 'ballistic' type and bring down both the pilot and aircraft together. The container is mounted in such a way that when the parachute is propelled from its container it will deploy without tangling with the aircraft structure. In spite of their glossy appearance ballistic parachutes also have to receive regular care and attention as specified by the makers.

Stopping your microlight blowing away

Microlights are really very light and can fly at low speeds, so they will easily blow over in a wind or even in the turbulence generated by larger aeroplanes and helicopters.

several of you are flying from a field or uncontrolled strip agree on a safe place for a store area and keep all the spare fuel there. Mark your containers with your name or aircraft identification and the type

The parachute is the pack on the side of the cockpit which the pilot has to deploy by hand. He rips open the cover and throws the packed parachute clear. It is attached to the trike and brings down both aircraft and pilot.

A parachute which brings down both aircraft and pilot. When fired the parachute is shot out of the tube and deploys clear of the aircraft structure.

If it is windy it is quick and easy to remove the wing. It takes a little longer to roll it up and put it in its bag where it will be completely secure.

A trike is simple to park securely. It is turned across wind with the into-wind wing pegged to the ground. If it is to be left for long the wheels should also be chocked.

When unattended they should be securely tied down from a strong point under each wing, and at the nose and tail.

Some microlights can be tipped nose down or have the nose wheel retracted to reduce the tendency of the wing to fly. Trikes can simply have the entire wing removed and laid on the ground or rolled up and put in its bag.

It is worth keeping three good-sized spiral pickets and lengths of nylon rope in a light bag (with a velcro strap or some other means of securing to the aircraft) for when you fly cross country. Do not use steel cable for picketing your aircraft as snatching in gusts causes shock loads on the wing structure.

If you do carry pickets, sleeping bags, etc., strapped to your microlight make sure that they are as near as possible to the aircraft's centre of gravity.

◀ If you land a tail dragger in a wind too strong to allow you to taxi, stay pointing into wind with the tail up until help comes.

▼ The result of gusts from a passing thunderstorm — three aircraft blew over. This two-seater Quicksilver was a new aircraft.

If your wing is not quickly detachable the whole aircraft should be securely picketed if there is any noticeable wind. This is an Easy Riser biplane.

8. Taking lessons

Because a microlight's construction looks so simple it is easy to think that it will be equally simple to fly, and that it is not necessary to have any lessons. This could be a big mistake. Although some people have taught themselves to fly and are still alive to tell the tale, once an aircraft is airborne there is no one to rescue the pilot except himself. If he is not fully prepared to act correctly he could be in big trouble; most 'pilot error' accidents are due to the pilot taking wrong decisions and flying beyond the limits of his experience.

If you have never flown before as a pilot, it is essential to go to a good microlight school or club* and be taught by a qualified instructor. But do not even rush into this without some careful thought. Flying, of any kind, is demanding of time and energy. To become a safe and competent pilot you have to fly regularly, so you need to decide how much time you can spare. It is even more important to decide *why* you want to fly. If it is something you have wanted to do for a long time but could never afford before microlights arrived, then go ahead

and learn. However, if you have no better reason than to keep up with your friends, it may be wiser to do something else.

For many people the decision to become a pilot is a big one, so it is only sensible to have one or two trial flights before you commit yourself. The best way to do this is in a 2-seat microlight with an instructor. If this is not possible a flight in a simple light aeroplane or a motor glider is better than nothing. Take time to make up your mind so that when you do

eventually begin you can concentrate on what you are doing without being disturbed by doubt.

If you are already an experienced aeroplane pilot do not be misled by the apparent simplicity of the microlight. It is certainly not difficult to fly, but it is much more susceptible to gusts and wind drift than a heavier, faster aeroplane. Don't be proud: take lessons with a qualified microlight instructor.

When you first arrive at the airfield carefully observe the flying. How long is the take-off run? Do some microlights climb more steeply than others? This is a Weedhopper shortly after take-off.

---

* Most National Aero Clubs or Microlight Associations will supply lists of clubs and schools.

First visit to a school

Before you become airborne you can learn a great deal by simply watching flying activities at a microlight airfield. How long is the distance to take off, how steeply do they climb, at what sort of height do they fly around the circuit, how much engine do they use when making an approach to land and, most important, how strong or gentle is the wind? When you have had a good look take steps to join the club or school; find out what it will cost, how instruction is given, and what types of aircraft are used.

There are still some schools which teach by the solo method which means that beginners are on their own from the start (page 115). It is a slower process than learning in a 2-seater and for most beginners more difficult, so it is assumed here that you will be learning dual on a 3-axis microlight with the instructor in the aircraft.

Air experience (familiarisation) flight

The purpose of this flight is to let you see how the aircraft is controlled and what the airfield and its surroundings look like from the air. The instructor may allow you to handle the controls for a few

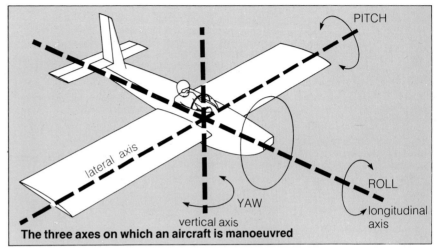

The three axes on which an aircraft is manoeuvred

Get the feel of sitting in an aircraft, and ask the instructor all the questions you want.

A two-seater Mistral on the approach. If you haven't flown a small aircraft before, have an 'air experience' flight before you commit yourself.

moments in the air. Try to pick a day when there are light winds and good visibility for this flight. You will probably find it difficult in the air to hear the instructor when he speaks, and you may find flying a microlight is so different from what you expected that you are still not sure about learning to fly them yourself. If so, ask to have another flight — or several more — so that you have time to become more familiar with all that is happening. Afterwards ask the instructor any questions you may have, and buy yourself a logbook in which to record details of your flights.

Log book
Apart from your own interest in having a record of all your flying and its highlights, such as your first solo, and later your first cross-country flight, you will not be able to gain your pilot proficiency certificate or licence unless you can produce evidence of your flying experience. It is sensible to have your log book signed by your instructor when you complete any stage of training, especially if you are likely to fly at another club or in another country.

LESSON 1 : The controls
Your first proper flying lesson will involve learning how to control the

When you start flying spend as much time as you can out on the field helping to move or park aircraft, so you quickly become familiar with microlight operations.

Look well ahead and learn the attitude for level flight and the correct airspeed. Try to keep the horizon in the right 'place'.

Attitude and speed correct

Too fast!

Nose too high —
airspeed too low

aircraft in the air: to fly at the correct airspeed and keep straight, and then to turn.

A car on the road moves in only one plane, i.e., directionally, when it turns either left or right, but an aircraft in the air moves in three planes:

Directionally — known as the yawing plane,

In pitch — when the nose is moved up or down, and

In roll — when the wings are raised or lowered laterally, and the aircraft banks.

To control your aircraft you have to be able to co-ordinate movement constantly in all three planes, and this will take considerable practice. For some time you may manage to keep the wings level only to find speed is increasing, or you may get the speed right but find you are no longer pointing in the same direction. Do not be discouraged. Everyone has these problems at the beginning until, quite suddenly, it all comes right. Always fly with the stick in your right hand.

Control of speed

At the start the instructor will teach you how to control the aircraft in pitch — which means control of airspeed. You know already that if the aircraft is flown too slowly — with the nose too high — it will stall. Conversely, you must not fly too fast — with the nose down — since not only could you exceed the maximum permitted speed for the aircraft, but you could soon arrive back on the ground. After the instructor has climbed the aircraft to a safe height he will adjust the *attitude* so that it is flying at the correct airspeed, and will then hand over control of speed to you. He will continue to look after roll and yaw. If there is an airspeed indicator (ASI) you will see the speed at which you are travelling through the air, probably something like 40 knots. Remember, if you move the stick forward the nose will go down and speed will increase; if you move it back the nose will rise and your airspeed will be reduced. You will soon discover that you need only gentle control movements to adjust the speed, and that you are receiving information through your ears as well as from the ASI. If you start to fly faster the noise will increase; if you decelerate the noise will lessen. Try to remember the noise level when the speed is correct. Look well ahead, and also around at the wings so as to learn the attitude at which the aircraft flies at the right speed. If you are perceptive you will soon learn the attitude at which the aircraft 'sits' in the air.

Move the stick gently forward, notice the effects of increasing

If one wing goes down the aircraft will start to turn in that direction.

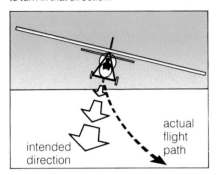

intended direction

actual flight path

speed, and return to the correct airspeed and level flight. Now raise the nose and see how this reduces the airspeed. Do not fly with the nose high for long as continuing deceleration will soon bring you close to the stall. Return to level flight. Repeat this exercise until you find it easy to return to the correct airspeed. Remember, a high-drag microlight decelerates quickly.

Keeping straight

Flying straight is really quite difficult to begin with because you not only have to control your airspeed but also keep the wings level. It is the first real lesson in co-ordination.

If you do not keep the wings level — or one wing goes down in a gust — the banked attitude the wings assume will cause the aircraft to start to turn, and this will change your direction. To return to straight flight you must bring the wings level again. You will now be flying

straight once more but no longer in the original direction. This will not matter while you are practising the exercise as the instructor is looking after the aircraft's position, but if you want to continue to fly in your original direction you will have to make a deliberate turn to get there.

LESSON 2:
Simple turns

An aircraft turns, or is returned to level flight, by using roll and yaw together. On a conventional 3-axis microlight this means using ailerons and rudder together. On a trike weight-shift produces roll, and the processes of roll induce yaw.

But whatever the control system an aircraft cannot be properly turned unless it is banked, and the rate of turn is controlled by the *amount* of bank. If the bank angle is 25 – 30° the turning circle will be larger than when the aircraft is more steeply banked. Rudder is used to prevent the banked aircraft slipping in towards the centre of the turn, or skidding outwards if too much rudder is used for the amount of bank.

To turn first check that you have sufficient airspeed. The stalling speed increases in a turn, although in a medium turn this is very little and you should in any case be flying with enough margin above

the stall to take care of ordinary turns. It is better not to complicate things by varying your speed at the same time as first learning to turn.

a Put on as much bank as you need, with a little rudder in the same direction to help you go smoothly into the turn.

b Continue the turn by maintaining the bank angle. If bank comes off the turn rate will lessen; if bank becomes steeper than you intend the rate of turn will increase and, unless you know how to hold the nose up, so will your airspeed.

c When you wish to come out of the turn level the wings, using a little rudder in the opposite direction to help you come out smoothly. Check airspeed.

Until you have had plenty of practice in co-ordinating the controls make only gentle to medium turns, and learn to do them smoothly. Steep turns are complex, and are dealt with later in Lesson 9 (see page 108).

Remember, pitch controls speed, and roll controls the bank which causes the aircraft to turn.

When you can do left and right medium turns you should be able to fly about in the air in control of airspeed, flying straight, and changing direction. Get as much practice as you can in co-ordination so that it gradually becomes instinctive and thus allows

Learning to fly on a trike does not take too long, but you should consider before you start if your ultimate objective is to stay on trikes or to eventually fly conventional aeroplanes.

To begin with the instructor may sit in front, but as he gains experience the student pilot will move into the front seat. For full dual the control frame will be fitted with a B-bar so that control is effective from both positions.

you time to see where you are and to look out for other aircraft.

With all this concentration you will probably have lost sight of the landing field, but don't worry, this is quite usual. While the instructor is taking you back to land you will have a few moments in which you can look around at the countryside and learn some local landmarks to help locate yourself.

Faults in turns

The usual faults in turns are *slipping* — having too much bank for the rate at which the aircraft is turning, and *skidding* — trying to turn using rudder with insufficient bank. You can discover this for

yourself. Go into a medium 30° turn and just increase bank. You will feel the aircraft slipping towards the lower wing tip while you, too, will slip in your seat. Return to a correct turn, and now increase rudder. You will feel the aircraft skidding uncomfortably out from the turn direction. Go back once more to a correctly made turn.

Learning to turn well is not difficult if you go at it one step at a time and practise often. It is very satisfying when you can make a good turn on every occasion.

A glider pilot learns this lesson quickly because he will fall out of thermals and soon find himself back on the ground unless he can turn properly.

LESSON 3: Climbing and gliding

So far you have learnt to co-ordinate the flying controls while generally flying level. However, to go up and come down you also have to control the power of your engine and relate it to airspeed.

Relationship between speed and power

It is easy to think when you open the throttle and feel a surge of power that power will always enable you to increase speed. Unfortunately, this is not so, because it is possible to achieve a situation where more power produces neither additional speed nor a better rate of climb. The attitude at which a glider flies is directly related to its airspeed, but for an aeroplane this may not be true. If you fly slowly with the nose high and then apply full power, the aircraft may not accelerate as you expect — a possibility which could easily arise if you temporarily throttle back while climbing, or the engine splutters and you apply or regain full power.

What happens is that your drag is much greater when you fly at a high angle of attack, and the power you have available is insufficient to accelerate the aircraft. This is known as 'flying on the backside of the drag curve'. If you find that full

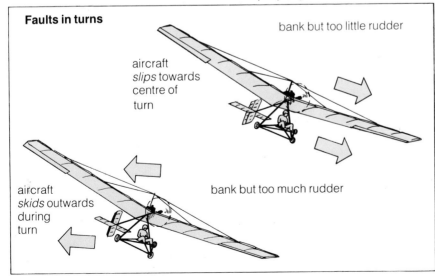

Faults in turns

bank but too little rudder

aircraft *slips* towards centre of turn

bank but too much rudder

aircraft *skids* outwards during turn

If you allow your aircraft to climb too slowly full power may not be enough to overcome the high drag. This happens easily if you climb too steeply after taking off.

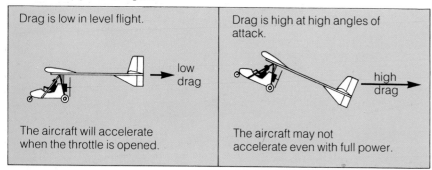

Drag is low in level flight.

low drag

The aircraft will accelerate when the throttle is opened.

Drag is high at high angles of attack.

high drag

The aircraft may not accelerate even with full power.

power is not getting you anywhere, lower the nose. If you throttle back you will make matters worse since any spare airspeed you have will soon disappear.

This is one more reason to learn the attitude at which your aircraft 'sits' in the air for normal cruise speed, and when gliding.

Climbing

To climb, the nose obviously has to be higher than in level flight and there should be enough power used to prevent any loss of speed. On a microlight this usually means full throttle.

The attitude for the best climb is quite precise: if the nose is too high the drag of the aircraft is increased and it will be impossible to maintain enough speed; if the nose is not high enough the aircraft's excessive speed will produce over-revving of the engine and almost no rate of climb. So, as well as using the controls to achieve the

correct attitude, you must use the throttle to achieve the correct speed.

Although you will have become used to the nose-up attitude of the climb when the instructor has been flying the aircraft you may find it more difficult to keep straight when doing it yourself. Try to pick out some landmark near the horizon, or even a cloud, to help you.

When you want to stop the climb and return to level flight lower the nose to the normal level flight attitude and reduce power to obtain the correct airspeed.

Gliding

When you close the throttle you become, in effect, a glider, and can obtain airspeed only through gravity. This means that you have to fly in a nose-down attitude steep enough to give you the airspeed you need. The rate at which you descend is determined by the glide ratio performance of your

aircraft: some microlights may be no better than 8:1, meaning that you can only fly a distance of 800 metres from a height of 100 metres (300 ft) — not very far. This may give you the distinct impression that you are coming down fast, which is true, but also that you could reduce the high descent rate by flying slower, which is untrue. If you do not have enough airspeed

From 1,000 ft without your engine you could be back on the ground in 3 minutes. If the engine stops get the nose well down QUICKLY, as high-drag microlights decelerate rapidly — which can only increase your rate of descent.

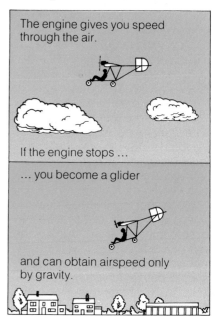

The engine gives you speed through the air.

If the engine stops ...

... you become a glider

and can obtain airspeed only by gravity.

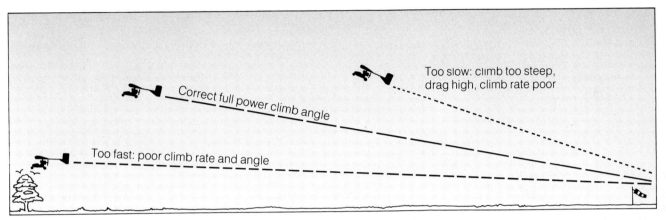

Too slow: climb too steep, drag high, climb rate poor

Correct full power climb angle

Too fast: poor climb rate and angle

you will not fly at all.

The only way you can improve the effective glide ratio of your aircraft is to use a small amount of power. This is a normal method of approaching in to land particularly if the wind is gusty.

At this stage the object of the lesson is to learn how your aircraft handles with the throttle closed, and to practise maintaining a steady airspeed. This will naturally be slightly lower than when flying level, power on, but it must be enough to give you a safe margin above the stall.

When gliding down the view ahead is even better because the nose is lower. Practise flying at the right attitude and airspeed without using the ASI, so that when you start to learn to land you will be able to concentrate on judging the approach without needing to look at the instruments. Listen to the sort of noise the aircraft makes when it is gliding at the correct approach speed.

Remember that if you come in to land too fast it will be difficult to put the aircraft neatly on the ground.

If you come in too slowly you will have :

a an increased rate of descent,
b insufficient speed to turn safely without stalling, and
c insufficient speed to land neatly — instead you will drop heavily onto the ground which will, at the very least, damage your pride.

LESSON 4: Taxiing

Taxiing gets you to the take-off position, and after landing returns you to the hangar or parking area. If this takes a long time because you cannot do it very well the engine may overheat or the plugs oil up. You will need to be able to taxi at a reasonable speed without anything going wrong.

When the instructor taxied the aircraft out it probably seemed easy, and in calm conditions it is, but in a wind it can become very difficult because the aircraft tries to weathercock into wind and away from the direction in which you want to go. Trikes are easier to taxi as the complete wing can be lowered into wind and there is no tail to encourage the weather-cocking effect. It is most important to taxi SLOWLY at first so that :

a you do not lose control,
b you can see where you are going, and
c you can stop quickly to avoid an obstruction.

Few microlights have brakes, even those with the pilot enclosed

Your first experience of being in charge of an aeroplane on your own is when you taxi about the ground. Do it slowly and give yourself plenty of room. Taxiiing along a slope close to bushes could land you in them unless you have learnt how to keep straight.

Taxiing on concrete or tarmac is more dificult in a crosswind than on grass. The tendency to weathercock into wind is considerable.

in a cockpit. If you are sitting in the open and you have a nosewheel you can obtain some braking effect by putting your boot on the steerable nosewheel, or, when going slowly, by putting your feet on the ground; however, be careful, particularly if the field slopes downhill. If your aircraft is a tail-dragger type it helps if it has a steerable tailwheel, although the usual way to taxi is to use rudder to turn. To make the rudder more effective give bursts of throttle to increase the airflow over its surface. Give yourself as much practice as possible.

Before leaving the parking area decide how you will reach your take-off place:

a If other aircraft are flying you must go round the edge of the field and not straight across it even when no aircraft are approaching at that moment. If a tyre bursts or your aircraft blows over you will be an obstruction for some time to come.

b Decide how the wind will affect you. If you have to taxi crosswind past other aircraft do so to windward, so that if you weathercock you will swing away from them.

Wind on the rudder surface weathercocks the aircraft into wind. Full downwind rudder may not be enough to keep straight if the wind is fresh.

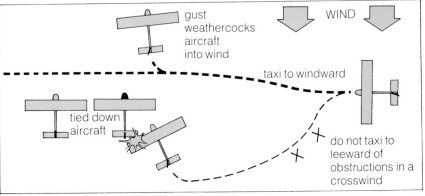

gust weathercocks aircraft into wind

WIND

taxi to windward

tied down aircraft

do not taxi to leeward of obstructions in a crosswind

Two up in a trike reduces the performance. This will lengthen the take-off run, and it will not climb as well after take-off as a single seater.

c If your seat is under the wing and you cannot see upwards make sure no one is coming in to land over the top of you.

d Decide where you will hold just before take-off to do your pre-take-off check.

If, when flying solo in a fresh wind, you find difficulty in taxiing back to the parking area, it is more sensible to taxi straight into wind until you are in the lee of the windward hedge. If this is not possible remain pointing into wind

with the engine running. Use the elevators to hold the tail in the air and wait for assistance. Attempting to taxi across a fresh wind will certainly mean some loss of control and may even result in the aircraft being blown over.

LESSON 5: Take-off and climb

Take-offs are made into wind because this reduces the ground run needed before becoming airborne. Supposing the speed at which your aircraft flies is 22 knots, then you will have to accelerate to

this speed on the ground when the air is calm. If, however, the wind into which your aircraft points blows over the wings at 12 knots, you will only need to accelerate to 10 knots over the ground to achieve the necessary airspeed of 22 knots to become airborne. So your ground run will be much less. If the wind were 22 knots you would, of course, have no ground run at all. On opening the throttle you would immediately take off.

If the first essential is to take off into wind, the next is to keep straight. On a marked runway this is fairly easy since you will soon see if you are diverging from the centre line, but on a featureless grass field it is easy to swing out of wind without noticing, particularly after you are airborne. So pick some tree or a church steeple in the distance upwind as a mark to aim for.

Taking off can be thought of in three stages:

a opening the throttle and accelerating to take-off speed;

b transferring the aircraft cleanly from the ground to the air; and

c climbing at the correct speed.

Before you open the throttle it is your responsibility to see that you will not get in the way of any aircraft coming into land. It is sensible, therefore, just before take-off to do your checks and then to turn the aircraft so that you can see whether anything is on the approach. If all is clear, turn into wind, open the throttle fully and hold it open. As the aircraft gathers speed keep it lightly on the ground by use of the elevator control until it feels buoyant and ready to fly. A quick glance at the airspeed indicator will confirm this. Keep looking well ahead. As the aircraft lifts from the ground do not let the climb steepen too soon. It is essential to build up airspeed. Only when you are sure you have *enough* should you ease the nose up and climb away. If the engine splutters lower the nose *immediately* so as not to lose airspeed. Check that you are still flying straight in the intended direction.

If the engine does not splutter, but stops after take-off, immediately lower the nose to a safe glide speed, and *close the throttle.* Look for the clearest space more or less ahead, and aim for it.

Never attempt to turn back into the field as you will almost certainly stall on the turn and crash. It is better to run into a hedge at a slow speed.

A good microlight climbs at a rate of about 500 ft/min, so in no wind you should, in theory, be at 500 ft after covering a horizontal distance of 3,000 ft (900 m). In a 10-knot wind you would be at 500 ft after a horizontal distance of only 2,000 ft (600 m).

In practice you may not climb as well as you expect because:

a the engine does not develop full power;

b you are flying in sinking air;

c you are climbing at the wrong speed; or,

d you have allowed the throttle to close partly.

For these reasons — and in case the engine cuts — ALWAYS give

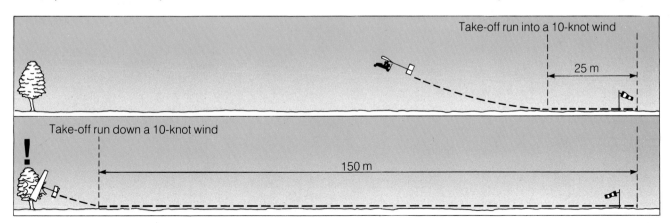

Take-off run into a 10-knot wind

25 m

Take-off run down a 10-knot wind

150 m

yourself the maximum length of take-off run that the field will allow.

When you have climbed to the height the instructor indicates, ease the nose down to the attitude for level flight and reduce power to obtain your normal cruise speed.

Failed take off

Apart from engine failure you may one day find the trees at the end of the field beginning to look disturbingly close, and the chance that you might not clear them very real. This could be because:

a your take-off run was longer than you expected,

b your rate of climb was poor, or

c you chose too small a field.

Whatever the reason you have only two alternatives:

a hope, and

b decide quickly to abandon the take-off.

There is no problem about abandoning the take-off as long as you decide in plenty of time. Close the throttle, get the nose down (if you are airborne) and land ahead. If a slight change of direction will give you a longer run make a gentle turn. Get the aircraft on the ground as soon as you can. Never rely on hope.

LESSON 6: Landing

A microlight is not difficult to land provided you are heading into wind, and this is not strong or gusty. It is simply a matter of gliding down at a suitable speed

Opposite:

1. A good landing comes from a good approach. Turn on to finals and get straight into wind with enough height to give you time to think and to adjust airspeed as necessary.

2. Nearing the ground. As you begin to flare for the landing, your airspeed will drop quite rapidly because the microlight is both high-drag and of small mass. Make sure you have enough airspeed to start with.

3. Microlights can cope with quite rough ground if they are landed properly. Keep straight and do not start holding off too high.

4. The correct landing attitude. Mainwheels touch followed by nose wheel as the aircraft decelerates. Don't aim to land on all three wheels at the same time, since the higher touch-down speed, combined with the usually heavier arrival, adds appreciably to wear and tear — and doesn't look good either.

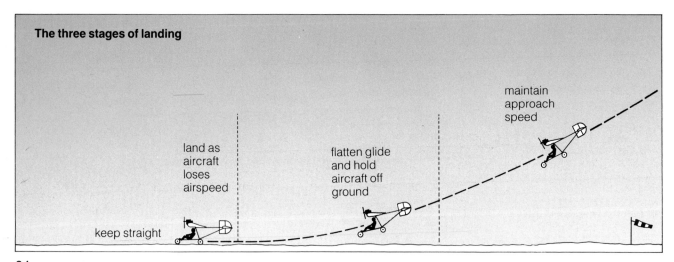

The three stages of landing

maintain approach speed

flatten glide and hold aircraft off ground

land as aircraft loses airspeed

keep straight

and, as the ground approaches, to flatten the glide angle so that when the aircraft is about a foot off the ground it is travelling parallel to it.

As the aircraft loses flying speed its three wheels settle on to the ground. The problems most beginners have are that they drift out of wind and they do not look far enough ahead. If you allow your eyes to focus on the grass as you pass over it you will tend to put the aircraft on the ground too fast — and since it may still have flying speed it will promptly bounce back into the air.

After landing *keep straight* until you stop. You do not know whether another pilot is landing near you. When the aircraft has stopped, turn left so as to look back and then taxi off the landing area if it is all clear.

Most microlights have tricycle undercarriages and these are easier to land than those with the third wheel at the back (tail draggers), although the ability to land a tail dragger with precision is very satisfying. With a tricycle undercarriage it is easy to become lazy about landings — until you start to fly in gusty air.

It is an old saying but a true one, that a good landing comes from a good approach. If you are not

straight into wind, or too low or too high, or have to make a low turn, you will be concentrating so much on getting the approach right that you will almost be on the ground before you are ready to land.

The landing really begins when you turn into wind on your final approach. If you are at a sensible height and properly lined up you can concentrate on:

a whether your airspeed is correct (beginners often come in to land too fast; only later when they develop confidence, or overconfidence, do they come in

too slowly);

b where you are likely to touch down, and if it is clear of obstructions;

c deciding when to hold off, or flare, for the landing.

For your first few landings it is better to come over the hedge on the high side and land well into the field. This avoids any worries about undershooting and also the visual distraction of trees and bushes flashing past close underneath.

Look well ahead — as though driving a car at about 50 mph on a straight road — and as the ground

Pathfinder on final approach, plenty of airspeed and nicely positioned to start the landing.

approaches gently ease back on the stick to flatten the glide and slowly lose speed. Do this progressively and do not rush it. As you get close to the ground continue keeping the aircraft just clear of the surface and wait for it to land itself. A good landing is one made on the main wheels and tail wheel, if a tail dragger, and the main wheels only, if a tricycle. Shortly after touching down the tricycle nose wheel should come down of its own accord.

If, during the landing, the aircraft does not keep straight, you are either out of wind, or you are flying with one wing low.

Power-on landings

If the wind is fresh you may have to make your approach with some power. You will need extra airspeed and about one-third power. Begin your hold off in the usual way and as you touch down throttle back. Keep straight. If you have a tricycle undercarriage you can hold the nose wheel firmly on the ground, but if you are flying a tail dragger it will pay to keep the tail up off the ground until you come to a stop. If the wind has become very strong try to keep the aircraft in this attitude until help arrives.

At the outset you should not fly in winds strong enough to make this technique necessary.

Crosswind landings

Although every effort should be made to touch down into wind every time, you will need to know what to do if, one day, you find the ground moving sideways just as you want to land. The first problems to recognise are:
a which way you are drifting, and
b what you can do about it.

If you know that you are going to have to land with some crosswind component make your final approach with the into-wind wing low. This will:
a cause you to slip slightly into wind, which helps to counteract the drift, and
b reduce the risk of the wind getting under the wing and cartwheeling you as you land.

The amount by which the wing can be held low will obviously depend on the ground clearance of the wing, and its span. Most high-wing microlights have plenty of clearance and so hitting the ground inadvertently with the wing tip is most unlikely.

Keep the into-wind wing low during the landing. After touch

Starting to reduce speed before landing.

Looking more closely at a good landing. The pilot has the stick fully back as he touches. The main wheels are down with the nose wheel following. The pilot's left hand is, correctly, on the throttle.

A trike about to land. The pilot is slightly high and a little slow, and will land with a higher descent rate than necessary.

down expect the aircraft to weathercock into wind — so do not land with obstructions close to the windward side!

If you discover, just as you are holding off, that you are drifting sideways there may only be enough time to kick on some *downwind* rudder. For example, if the wind is blowing from the left and is causing you to drift to the right put on right rudder. All this does is to help point the aircraft in the direction in which it is going, so that when the wheels touch they will act as wheels and not dig in sideways. Keep the aircraft firmly on the ground; if it bounces the drift will be worse at the next arrival. Try to keep the into-wind wing low. Again, as you slow down on the ground the aircraft will want to weathercock into wind.

LESSON 7:
The circuit

Up to now almost all your flying has concentrated on handling the aircraft, while your instructor has been taking the decisions — when to take off, how high to climb, when to turn towards the landing field, and when to start gliding down. Now *you* have to start taking these important decisions which are an essential part of becoming a pilot. You can already take off, fly about in the air, and land; now you need to start planning how to position yourself in the air so that you can fly to an airfield and land on it. The first step is the circuit.

There are two reasons for having an organised pattern which all pilots use when flying around an airfield: firstly it makes the planning of the approach easier for the pilot, and secondly, it reduces the risk of collision.

The basic circuit forms a rectangle diagrammatically, consisting of the climb out, a crosswind leg, a downwind leg, a second crosswind leg (known as the base leg), and a final approach into the wind for the landing. If you have not taken off from the field, but are arriving from a cross-country flight, the best position from which to join the circuit is at the beginning of the downwind leg. As you approach you can clearly see all aircraft flying in the circuit and can adjust your flight path accordingly. At a busy airfield it is conventional to join the circuit on the unused or 'dead' side.

A microlight circuit, made at perhaps 30–40 knots airspeed, is obviously smaller than that needed for faster aircraft, and it also does not have to be flown at so great a height. 500 ft is normally high enough at the start of the downwind leg.

If other aeroplanes fly from the

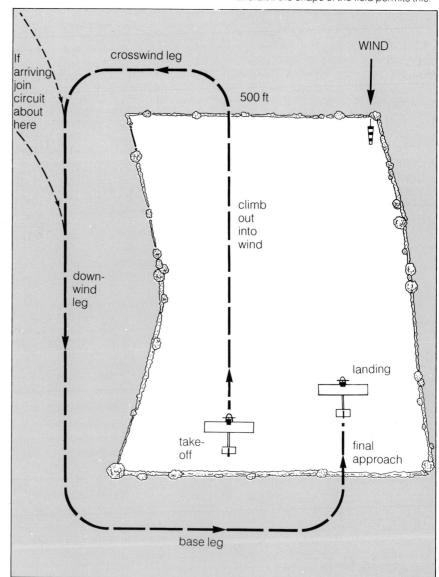

If arriving join circuit about here

crosswind leg

WIND

500 ft

climb out into wind

down-wind leg

landing

take-off

final approach

base leg

same field it will be safer and more economical if the microlights fly to a special pattern. It is the responsibility of the pilot to find out what this is before arriving. But first of all you must learn about the basic circuit.

a *Climb out* The objective is to reach a height of 400–500 ft directly upwind of the take-off point, and a little distance upwind of the field. If the wind is fresh this height will be reached closer to the upwind boundary than if there is no wind.

b *First crosswind leg* Turning crosswind enables you to see the airfield and where you aim to land on it, and also to assess the extent of the wind drift. If there is no wind you will travel over the ground in the same direction as the nose of the aircraft is pointing. In a wind you will end up downwind of the line along which you think you are flying — unless you correct by crabbing across wind.

When the aircraft is a little beyond the end of the upwind boundary of the field it should be turned onto:

c *The downwind leg* This is the main planning leg of the circuit. The landing area and the approach path leading to it should be studied to see what other aircraft — or cars or dogs — are likely to obstruct your

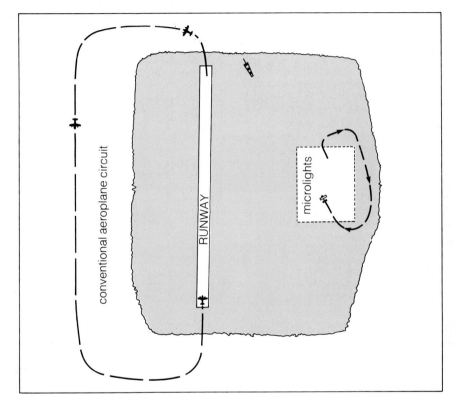

touch-down. The windsock should be checked for wind strength, and any change in direction — it sometimes changes quickly. Your height should be checked. Are you higher than you expected, or lower? Is your airspeed correct?

The downwind leg should be used to maintain height or lose it gradually by reducing engine power.

When operating at an airfield with other traffic, it is better if microlights have their own marked landing area and fly opposite-hand circuits. Take care not to drift over the runway if there is a crosswind blowing towards it. On some airfields it may be better for microlights to make a smaller lower circuit in the same direction as the larger aircraft. Find out the arrangements before you visit.

This is the leg on which a conventional aeroplane pilot would lower his undercarriage. Most microlights are not so sophisticated, but if you later buy one with retractable wheels this is the time to ensure that you have them for landing on.

If the wind is fresh your speed over the ground on this leg will be higher than your airspeed, so

Ahead of you is an airfield. Do you know how to join the circuit, where to find the signals square, and where to land? You should not start to fly across country until you do know.

it is easy to drift downwind of the airfield.

d The turn on to *Base leg* should be made only a short distance downwind of the landing field boundary, and your height should now be about 300 ft. The base leg is used to make final corrections for drift and height. Make sure that sufficient airspeed is available to deal with turbulence, wind gradient, or to turn to avoid other aircraft.

A good look-out is essential,

particularly downwind of the airfield, for microlights coming in low on an airliner-type approach. Such approaches are often made, but are bad practice as any engine problem guarantees an emergency landing.

On reaching a position directly downwind of the landing place you should turn into wind to line up for the final approach. If you have enough height glide in with the throttle closed, but if there is any risk at all of undershooting use engine so that you will reach the airfield *and* have sufficient airspeed. You should aim to touch down about a third of the field length in from the boundary.

As the aircraft nears the ground it should be held off and landed in the usual way.

When you start to fly circuits and have to take each of the many decisions as to when and where to turn, keep a good look-out for other aircraft, and constantly assess wind drift, you will discover that it is more difficult to fly accurately. So many demands are being made on your concentration that something inevitably gets left out. Just make sure it is not airspeed, as without enough you will not stay in the air. This is why, when you start flying circuits, it is sensible to use an organised pattern, even if you are the only aircraft in the air.

Overshooting, or going round again

Sometimes when you come in to land you will be baulked by another aircraft whose pilot appeared to take off without looking for microlights on the approach. You have two possible courses of action: to swerve to one side and land, or to open the throttle, climb up, and go around for another landing.

The latter is the sensible method. It is safe and it gives you plenty of time to make another approach. Swerving at low height and at low airspeed may either dump you on the ground or put you in the path of yet another pilot coming in to land.

It is important to take the decision to go round again as early as possible. Do not dither in the hope that the aircraft causing the problem will just disappear. As soon as you decide to go round again:

a open the throttle fully and check that your airspeed is enough to allow you to climb;

b climb straight ahead until you are clear of the airfield boundary and are in the usual circuit pattern;

c reduce power to normal cruise, turn cross wind, and survey the situation (you will probably be higher than usual at this stage of the circuit); and,

d fly the circuit adjusting height so

104

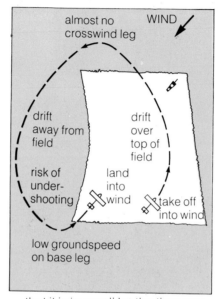

almost no crosswind leg

WIND

drift away from field

drift over top of field

risk of under-shooting

land into wind

take off into wind

low groundspeed on base leg

that it is 'normal' by the time you turn on to your base leg.

Crosswind circuits

If microlights fly from a grass field the circuit can shift round as needed to align with the wind. If, however, you fly from a narrow strip, or from an airfield at which larger aircraft are using a runway, the circuit may have a consider-able crosswind component. Provided you can do the actual take off and landing into wind, the effects of this on the conventional left-hand circuit will be:

Wind from the right

a to drift you over the airfield on

When there is a crosswind the flight path of a microlight over the ground will be like these examples if the pilot makes no correction for drift. You should fly crabbing into the wind so that you track along the desired path over the ground.

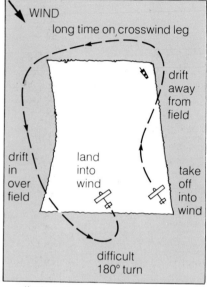

WIND

long time on crosswind leg

drift away from field

drift in over field

land into wind

take off into wind

difficult 180° turn

climb out,

b to give you a fast crosswind leg,

c to drift you away from the airfield on the downwind leg, and

d to give you low ground speed on your base leg.

The combined effect of **c** and **d** will make it easy to undershoot. Be prepared for this.

Wind from the left

a to drift you away from the airfield on climb out,

b to give you a slow crosswind leg,

c to drift you in towards the airfield on the downwind leg, and

d as a result leave you insufficient

space in which to fly your base leg.

Consequently you may have to make a turn of almost 180° to get into wind. This will make it difficult to judge:

a when to make the turn, and

b whether or not you are exactly into wind for the landing.

None of these problems need arise if you appreciate the extent to which you may drift, and compensate for it by crabbing across wind so that you still fly the desired path over the ground.

LESSON 8: Stalling

Most people realise that if airspeed is lost an aircraft will stall. What the pilot needs to understand most of all is how to avoid stalling by mistake.

We know that a wing generates enough lift to support the weight of the aircraft only when the airflow over it is moving fast enough. On a lightly loaded microlight wing this minimum airspeed is low, around 20–22 knots, whereas on a highly loaded military fighter it is perhaps 100 knots.

To generate lift most efficiently the wing is carefully shaped (its wing profile or section) and must meet the airflow at a certain angle (the angle of attack). On a microlight with an 'aeroplane' wing this angle is about 5°, and on a trike

Most stalling problems are caused because the pilot did not realise he was flying too slowly. This can easily happen on the approach if the pilot is undershooting, or on the climb-out – in a misguided attempt to clear the trees! This pilot did not hurt himself but his aircraft was badly broken getting it down.

it is a little higher. If the angle of attack is increased this, to begin with, generates more lift — and also more drag. If it is increased further, drag continues to increase but a point is soon reached at which the airflow over the wing becomes turbulent and the wing ceases to generate enough lift to support the aircraft. This is the stall. The angle of attack at which a microlight wing stalls is about 15°.

However, you will not increase the angle of attack at which your wing stalls only by raising the nose skywards. What counts is the angle

at which the airflow meets the wing. If you are pulling sharply out of a dive the stalling angle could be reached while the nose is still low. And you can stall the wings in a steep turn if you are flying slowly (see page 108).

You need to be able to recognise the symptoms which indicate that the aircraft is about to stall. Most stalling accidents occur because the pilot was unaware he was flying too slowly — at too high an angle of attack — and then, when the aircraft did stall, he was so surprised that he failed to take

corrective action in time.

In the two-seater the instructor will show you the stall at a safe height and how to recognise it. You will learn that when the aircraft is being flown near the stall:

a the nose is higher than usual, with the horizon lower in relation to the cockpit or your feet;

b your rate of descent is increasing even though the nose is high;

c noise is reduced, or different;

d the controls feel sloppy (e.g. if you move the stick, reaction to it is slow); and,

e the airflow on your face is less.

At any time you notice one or more of these symptoms, get the nose down and gain airspeed. If you do not, the aircraft will stall. When flying straight the stall is usually gentle on a microlight, with enough airspeed being regained almost as soon as the nose has dropped a little. It does not seem dangerous, but do not be misled.

The spin

If an aircraft is stalled in a turn, or with rudder on, it can start to spin. On a microlight this may happen readily because of the small margin above the stall at which it often flies. In a turn only the fuselage is flying at the indicated airspeed, the outer wing is flying faster, while the inner wing is flying slower. This inner wing tip may be

To begin with it may be quite difficult to get the attitude of the climb right. Trikes can climb at an apparently very steep attitude and you may feel lost without the horizon ahead of you.

very close indeed to the stall speed in even a moderate turn. Inadvertent stalling from a turn occurs most often during the approach to land, because the pilot is concentrating on other things, instead of making sure there is *enough airspeed*. Because of the many different control systems on microlights it is not as easy to give a set of routine actions for spin recovery as it is for a conventional aeroplane or glider.

What the pilot must try to do, in this order, is:

a stop the rotation,
b unstall the wings by gaining speed, and
c recover to normal flight without gaining a dangerously excessive speed — or losing too much height — in the process.

If you recognise in time that the aircraft is about to spin, get the nose down. Do not try to hold up a dropping wing with aileron or

If you want to find out how the aircraft responds when flown close to the stall, or you want to do some stalls to learn how to recover with the minimum loss of height, give plenty of space between you and the ground. 1,000 ft or more is sensible, as your rate of descent increases when flying near the stall and you may not notice how rapidly you are nearing the ground.

spoileron. Obviously there are occasions when engine power can be used to ward off an incipient stall or to help recovery, because it can quickly contribute speed, as well as more airflow over tail control surfaces. However, it is no substitute for flying with enough airspeed. If the aircraft is stalled close to the ground, using engine could be a mistake.

LESSON 9: Understanding the turn

So far your turns have probably been little more than simple changes of direction to help you fly around the circuit. But if you now go to a safe height and try to fly continuous 360° circles you may discover all sorts of interesting things start to happen. The most usual is that both bank and speed increase, yet when you pull the stick back to reduce speed the turn merely tightens and speed increases still further. Soon you

can be spiralling earthwards, probably with the engine screaming as well.

The load the wings have to carry is greater during a turn than in straight flight. This is because they have to counteract centrifugal force as well as support the weight of the aircraft. When making a turn, therefore, the lift on the wings has to be increased. This is achieved by flying faster or by flying at a

A correct turn is made by controlling the required amount of bank, and by maintaining the desired airspeed.

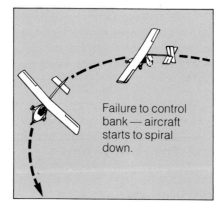

Failure to control bank — aircraft starts to spiral down.

higher angle of attack — usually a bit of both. In gentle turns the extra speed needed is not significant, but at 60° of bank — about as steeply as a microlight can be turned — the stalling speed increases 1.4 times, i.e. if it is 20 knots in straight flight it goes up to 28 knots in the turn. Because of this increased load on the wing the engine power required to obtain the same speed as in straight flight will be greater. In an under-powered microlight it may not be possible to do a steep turn without losing height.

Remember that on a slow-flying aircraft of moderate to large span the inner wing in a steep turn may be very close to stalling, even though the speed has been increased.

In a steep turn it is even more important to control the bank than in a gentle one. It is when you permit the bank to increase more than is necessary that things start to go wrong. Remember, when an aircraft is banked it tends to slip in the direction of the lower wing, so you have to use rudder in the same direction to prevent slip; but, when you are steeply banked, both bank and rudder are turning you in the direction of the lower wing, and in a steep turn that is downwards. This is why your speed increases. To fly at the speed you want while at the same time keeping the nose of the aircraft moving steadily around the horizon, you need backward pressure on the stick.

When you start to fly steeper turns begin with a few circles at an angle of bank with which you are familiar, and observe what happens and what control inputs you are actually making. Then increase the angle of bank to about 40°–45° and fly a few more circles. You will discover that you are having to make a conscious effort to avoid the speed increasing, and that you are flying a circle of smaller radius. When you can make 40° turns neatly, increase bank to 45°–50° and repeat the exercise. You may find 50° as steep as you can control without losing height or gaining too much speed.

If at any time you find your turn getting out of control *take off bank*, return to level flight and begin again.

Before starting to practise steeper turns, check that you have

a enough height (about 2,000 ft is sensible);

b had a good look round for other aircraft;

c a good clear horizon to use as reference; and

d enough extra airspeed for the steepness of the turn you intend to execute.

When you want to come out of the turn, level the wings, using

opposite rudder at the same time, and check airspeed. You may find on coming out of a steep turn that the nose is high and you are too slow.

Sideslipping

Unless your aircraft is fitted with spoilers, airbrakes, or flaps to help steepen the glide path when coming in to land, you need to know how to sideslip. Unfortunately, you will only be able to sideslip

effectively on a full 3-axis control microlight which has ailerons or spoilerons if the aircraft has a powerful rudder. On a high-drag microlight with no 'fuselage' it may not be easy to sideslip effectively at all.

The object of sideslipping is to worsen the drag of the aircraft by presenting it partly sideways to the airflow, so that the performance is degraded and the sink rate increased. It is most useful on the

If you find yourself doing steep turns at this height examine your motives. Overconfidence and aviation do not go well together.

final approach into wind; but do not continue sideslipping close to the ground.

The aircraft can be made to sideslip by flying with *opposite* aileron and rudder. Fly at normal approach speed with the throttle closed, and put on, for example, left bank and right rudder. The bank lowers the left wing and the rudder swings the nose to the right. The objective on an approach is to swing the nose out of wind sufficiently to balance the slip in the opposite direction so that the path over the ground continues to

be straight into wind. This is more difficult to do on some aircraft than others, usually because the rudder is not powerful enough to counteract the slip. Practise — at a safe height — until you find the right balance. You will probably need to use some back pressure on the stick as well to keep the nose up.

To stop the sideslip, take off rudder and bank, and check airspeed since you may come out nose high, or pointing in the wrong direction. This is difficult to do well at first.

The slipping turn

If you are higher than you want to be on a glide approach you can increase your rate of descent by making your turn onto base leg and onto finals with too little rudder for the bank. This will cause the aircraft to slip, which increases its drag. It is a useful and safe manoeuvre, provided it is not done at too low a height.

9. Rules of the air

Now that you can take off, fly around the field and land back safely you are almost a pilot — even though you have not yet flown solo. But before you fly on your own, you have to learn the rules for avoiding collision, and a few others about low flying and, later, for avoiding prohibited airspace.

Avoiding collision

As on the road and at sea, the rules of the air enable pilots to act in a certain way — to avoid hitting each other. They are vital and you should learn them well, so that if you do have to take action quickly you will not waste seconds working

out what you ought to do — it should be as instinctive as stopping at a red traffic light on the roads. The rules are as follows:

Meeting head on
When flying towards another aircraft or nearly so, both pilots turn away to their right.

Converging courses
When aircraft are converging, the one which has the other on its right GIVES WAY. If *you* have to give way it is often safer to turn to fly behind the other aircraft.

Overtaking
It is the responsibility of the overtaking aircraft to keep clear, and you should overtake on the right of the aircraft you wish to pass. (When ridge soaring, gliders and hang gliders may pass each other on either side.)

Coming in to land
The lower aircraft has right of way.

General
Although powered aircraft should give way to gliders and balloons, it is the responsibility of *every* pilot to

The law says that an aircraft shall not fly in formation with another without prior agreement. The helicopter is still some distance from the Weedhopper, but if it comes close its downwash could make the microlight uncontrollable.

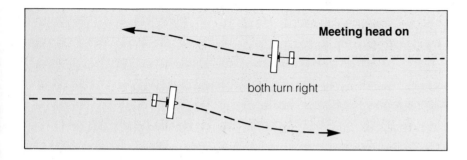

Meeting head on

both turn right

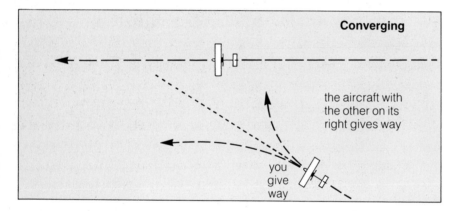

Converging

the aircraft with
the other on its
right gives way

you
give
way

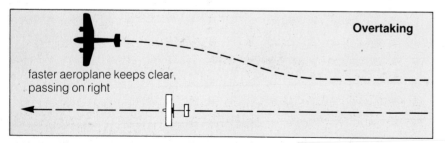

Overtaking

faster aeroplane keeps clear,
passing on right

The rules for avoiding collision. Sometimes, when you find yourself converging with another aircraft and you have to give way, it is better to turn towards it so that you will pass astern. If you turn in the same direction as the other aircraft you may put it in your blind spot.

do *everything possible* to avoid a collision.

You may not fly in formation with another aircraft without prior agreement with its pilot.

When there is 1,000 ft of nothing between you and the ground it is obviously not sensible to make a bold stand for your rights. Keep a good look-out and anticipate the possibility of a collision long before you need to take action.

Low flying

Low flying is fun but it has four disadvantages:

a the noise you make is unnecessarily disturbing for people on the ground;

b you may not see power wires in time;

c it can be hazardous if the engine stops; and,

d it is against the law, which says that you must not:

- Fly over towns below a height which would enable you to land clear of the area, or below 1,500 ft above the highest fixed object within 2,000 ft.

- Fly over or within 1,000 yds of any open-air assembly of more than 1,000 persons.

- Fly closer than 500 ft to any person, vessel, vehicle, or structure.

- The only exemption is when you are taking off or landing.

Airfield traffic zones

Each airfield has a traffic zone up to 2,000 ft above it and within 1.5 nautical miles of its boundaries. You must keep clear unless you are going to land. On entering the zone you must make a left-hand circuit, unless directed otherwise, and you must keep clear of low cloud. Before going to a strange airfield you should learn and obey the Airfield Signals so that you do not cause confusion.

General safety

You may not drop anything from an aircraft except:

a persons by parachute in an emergency (including yourself);

b articles for the purpose of saving life, such as a sleeping bag to someone stranded on a mountain;

c ballast in the form of water or fine sand (pilots of gas balloons do this); and,

d tow ropes on an airfield.

You may not carry a passenger other than in a proper seat designed for the purpose, and you may not carry dangerous goods, such as toxic fluids or explosives.

Low flying may be fun, but it annoys people on the ground and it is illegal. What would you do if the engine stopped?

113

If you are navigating by following a motorway, canal, etc, you must do so keeping it on your left.

Night
Night officially begins half an hour after sunset and ends half an hour before sunrise as observed on the ground. Does your insurance cover night flying?

Accidents
You must report any accident which causes injury or substantial damage without delay to the police and to BMAA or the CAA Accident Investigation Branch (AIB).

Signals
There are many signals which you will need to learn before you fly across country — as well as rules about controlled airspace (see page 159) — now is the time to learn the meaning of all those shapes in the standard airfield signals square.

Airfield signals
Signals may be displayed in a special square or out on the airfield.

Take-offs and landings to be parallel to the shaft of the T and towards the cross arm.

The direction of take-offs and landings may not be the same. The equivalent ground signal is a black ball hanging from a mast.

Area of the airfield to be used only by light aircraft.

Helicopter landing area.

Right-hand circuit in force. (All circuits left-handed unless this is displayed.)

Glider flying is in progress. The equivalent ground signal is two red balls from a mast.

Aircraft are confined to runways and paved surfaces.

Take-offs and landings to be made on the runway. Taxiing on the grass permitted.

Light aircraft may fly from the runway or from a special light-aircraft area.

Landing area boggy or in poor state. Take special care.

Airfield is unsafe. Landings prohibited.

The section marked is unfit for use.

10. Flying solo

First solo

If you have learnt to fly 'dual' you will have become used to depending on your instructor in the air. He, of course, will have been trying to get you to take decisions for yourself. Then, one day, he will have to get out of the two-seater and send you off on your own — *solo*. Although it may not be apparent, the instructor will have chosen this moment carefully; he will be satisfied that not only will you be able to fly competently around the airfield and land back, but that you should be able to cope with possible emergencies, such as engine failure. He will also have checked that the weather is suitable: not windy, air reasonably smooth, and visibility good so that there is a clear horizon to help you fly at the right attitude and speed.

The first solo usually consists of three circuits and landings. The first is proof for you that you can do it, the second is to prove the first was not just luck, and the third is to give you the chance to improve on the first two.

The first solo is a great moment in any pilot's career, but you are on your own now, and it is up to you whether you improve your flying and develop the skills and judgement that mark an experienced, able flier. Talk to the best pilot you can find and he will tell you he is still learning.

Training solo

Some schools train new pilots solo right from the very beginning. It takes longer to learn, and the weather has to be just right; but if these limitations are accepted and you have time to spare it is possible to learn this way.

Slow, light microlights, such as the Eagle, are used, and for the

You can learn a great deal just talking to experienced pilots, as well as those who are at the same stage of learning as you are and are coming across the same problems. Discussing your bad landings could give you just the clue you wanted.

The Eagle is still popular because it is slow, light, and easy to fly. It is quite good for local flying while building up air time.

Flying a two-seater solo. Most need ballast with only one pilot aboard, otherwise the c.g. will be too far aft and the aircraft will be unstable. On the Duet ballast is carried in the transverse tube built into the nose.

first few lessons you will probably be towed across the airfield by a car. This enables the instructor, driving the car, to adjust the speed very precisely. He can tow you at less than flying speed while you become familiar with the controls and practise keeping straight. After a few runs like this he will tow you a little faster so that you fly just clear of the ground. You can then practise using the elevator to take off, fly along at a height of about 2 metres, and then land. If you make a mistake and climb too high the instructor will slow the car so you subside back on the grass.

In between tows he will tell you if and where you went wrong and will brief you for the next tow. When he is satisfied that you understand how to make low hops and are developing good co-ordination, he will dispense with towing and let you have control of the engine. Now you practise doing exactly the same height of hop as before, using the throttle to get you off the ground and let you down again.

You will probably be delighted at being let off the lead and allowed to be master of your own fate, but all your instructor has given you is responsibility for yourself, not the ability to fly. So take it easy and go on making straight hops up to perhaps 50 ft until you can do them well every time.

The next step is to climb a little

higher after take-off, close the throttle as you get the nose down, and glide at a steady approach speed. Follow it with a correctly flared landing, not just an arrival on all three wheels. You may find it difficult to glide down at the correct attitude and speed as you seem to be back on the ground so quickly. Your instructor can help you by holding up the tail of your aircraft while you sit in the seat looking well ahead, before you take off. Practise making straight hops as high as is practicable without running out of airfield.

After this do some deliberate gentle turns. You will almost certainly have found yourself turning without meaning to, so all your efforts will have been concentrated on getting straight into wind again. You will now still

have to get back into wind for the landing which really means two gentle turns — in the form of a slim 'S'.

It is better to do these flights with a light wind rather than in calm air, as you want to have enough height to complete the turns before you arrive back on the ground. The objective is to teach yourself to control the aircraft accurately at the different attitudes and speeds for climb, level flight, glide, and to flare for the landing. Don't just let the aircraft waffle into the air and flop back on the ground again.

The problem with solo training is that you cannot progress very far without coming to the end of the airfield, so you have to go from high hops to flying a complete circuit of the airfield in one jump. This means many new things have to be tried out — and learnt — all at the same time, which is undesirable in any form of aviation. You can help yourself to make your first circuits safely by:

a carefully watching other pilots fly circuits and observing where they turn, how high they fly, and how much engine they use;

b having a flight in a light aeroplane with the pilot simulating a microlight circuit as nearly as possible, so you can see what the airfield looks like as you fly around it;

c obtaining a thorough briefing from your instructor and asking questions until you are absolutely clear as to what you are trying to do; and

d flying your first circuit in a light wind with good visibility.

The biggest difficulty on your first circuit will probably be knowing when to come out of your turns. In general, you will only need to change direction by 90° to turn on to the next leg of the circuit, so before you start to turn look in that direction and pick some landmark, e.g. white house, lake etc., which is beyond the wingtip. Do your gentle turn and come out when you are pointing towards it. Keep the landing field in sight at all times and NEVER turn away so that you cannot see it.

If there is some wind you may think you are flying too fast on the downwind leg. This is because your speed over the ground is faster than your airspeed. Do not be tempted to reduce airspeed or you could leave yourself with too little.

When you make your final turn into wind everything should look familiar once more — provided you are not undershooting. Aim to land in the middle of the field.

Once you have made a few circuits successfully you can begin to build up your airtime and your experience as a pilot. But take it slowly and do not permit yourself to become over-confident. Never try anything new — steeper turns, gustier winds, poorer visibility, or short field landings — until you can carry out what you are already doing with precision. Your instructor will give you practice in emergency procedures, such as action in event of engine failure, so you will have plenty to do. And teach yourself to look out for other aircraft in the air; solo trained pilots are usually worse in this respect than those taught in dual aircraft.

Local flying — gaining experience

Until you have at least 15 hours flying experience, preferably more, you should fly only locally, within sight and 8 nautical miles of your home field. This will allow you an excellent opportunity to develop a whole range of skills, provided you give yourself an objective on every flight and try to carry it out well. For some you will need the co-operation of your instructor, but others you can do by yourself. For example:

1 You can climb to a safe height and practise continuous medium turns in both directions. Many pilots turn better in one direction than in the other, but you should not consider yourself a good pilot until you can do both left and right circles equally well.

2 Climb on a clear day to several thousand feet without going into cloud or becoming disorientated. If you have only flown at about 500–600 ft so far do not go high straight away. Maybe even 1,000–2,000 ft is enough to begin with.

3 Go to a safe height and deliberately try to fly very close to the stall, but without actually stalling. Practise this with power, and as a glider. Make sure you do not get lower than you mean to inadvertently, since your aircraft's descent rate will be higher when you are flying close to the stall.

4 Go to about 1,000 ft upwind of the landing field, close the throttle and fly the circuit as a

glider so that you land where you had intended on the field. Make sure your engine does not stop: if it does not like being run slowly give it a small burst of throttle at intervals to keep it warm. If you find you are undershooting, use power in plenty of time to reach the landing field safely. Work out why your approach was misjudged — was the wind stronger than you expected, were you flying at the wrong airspeed, or did you just think your aircraft would perform better than it did? Repeat the

exercise with more proficiency next time.

5 Stay in the air for longer than you have done so far, perhaps for 1 hour or 1½ hours. Work out beforehand:
a if you have enough fuel:
b if you are wearing sensible, warm clothes;
c whether you might need any food (e.g. chocolate), or drinking water;
d how you are going to use the time usefully; and,
e if the weather is going to remain reasonable.
Remember that if you get cold

or tired you will fly less competently, so it is better to land early; try flying for a longer period of time on another day.

6 On a day with good visibility fly further from the landing field than you have done before, without getting lost, and for not more than 8 n.m. (14.8 km). Fly to a prominent landmark perhaps 10 km distance away, turn around it and fly in a straight line back to the airfield; or, fly a similar distance along a motorway or canal — keeping it on your left — and then return along it directly, or via a prominent landmark which lies a little to one side. The objective here is to learn to recognise your airfield and other landmarks from different viewpoints, and also to become familiar with the area around your home base. This is important before you start flying in poorer visibility.

7 When you are beginning to feel confident that you can handle your microlight with reasonable accuracy and judgement you will be ready to practise flying in stronger or gustier winds, or on days when active thermals

When you are putting in solo time you will not have an instructor around to advise you. Look after yourself — and don't take off too close to standing crops or hedges.

Flying from farm fields is delightful —
provided you have permission and you have
walked over the field to find if it is big
enough, and if it is free of potholes.

are present. The objective is
not to prove that your microlight
can be flown in rougher
weather, but to teach yourself
how to recognise and cope with
drift, wind gradient on the
approach, and continuous
moderate turbulence in the air.
Do not experiment on days with
squalls or thunderstorm
development. If thermals are
well organised and reasonably
large, climb to about 1,500–
2,000 ft, reduce power and try
to find and stay in the lift by
circling. You will soon notice
that as you enter a thermal its
energy will give you temporary
increase in airspeed as well as
pushing the nose up; but as
you fly out of a thermal you will
lose energy and airspeed —
watch for this.
The occasions when you will need
help from your instructor include:

When following a railway, road or river keep
it on your left.

1 Landing at a different field.
Your instructor will almost
certainly have an arrangement
with a farmer for an emergency-
use field, and will brief you
when you are ready to attempt
an away landing, how to plan
your approach, and how you
will return home. The instructor
may wish to fly your aircraft out
himself, or it may be retrieved
by car.

2 The next stage in practising
away landings is to combine
one with a navigational
exercise. Your instructor will
specify the route for you to fly
— perhaps a local triangular
course of 25 km — and where
you have to land. It is likely to

be the same field in which you
landed for the previous
exercise, but probably with a
different wind direction. This
time *you* should take off again
from the field, so:
a get a general briefing from
your instructor,
b do not forget to do your
pre-take-off check, and
c use the *full length* of the field
for your take-off run.

3 Precision landings. Your
instructor will put out a spot on
the landing field on which he
will expect you either to touch
down, or to finish your landing
run. The object is not to hit the
spot by throwing the aircraft at
the ground, but to develop your

Overconfidence is a fruitful source of accidents. What happens if this pilot's engine stops? He is only 100 ft up.

difficult. The control responses are the same, though the handling may not be so light or quick. On take-off some trikes need to be lifted off the ground with a moderately large control input, which then has to be adjusted fairly quickly so that the climb does not become too steep and slow. With little except your feet — instead of your head — in front for assessing the attitude of the aircraft in relation to the horizon, it is not particularly easy to get this right to begin with.

What the hang-glider pilot needs to learn and practise are the aspects of flying which are different from those he is used to. They include:

a taking off and landing on wheels;

b keeping straight during the take-off run;

c climbing with power (different from climbing in thermals);

d freedom from being tied to a ridge and its lift band (easy to become lost if this point is not appreciated);

e appreciating that 'airspeed' and 'attitude' are not synonymous when power is used; (see p.84)

f appreciating that the engine can stop at any time (and if it does the inevitable forced landing will be more difficult than for a hang glider); and,

g appreciating that the freedom to wander carries with it

skill in landing exactly where you want, and doing so as neatly as possible. He may also set up precision landing competitions so that you will be able to compare your accuracy with that of other pilots. You should, of course, form a habit of deciding where you will land before every take-off or whenever you join the circuit, and of seeing how close you can get to your chosen spot.

It is at this stage of your flying career that you should get yourself into the air as often as you can, to consolidate everything you learn. If you fly infrequently you may forget a considerable amount of what you did a month ago, and so have to re-learn it all over again. This is wasteful of time and money, and if it results in making little progress can be wasteful of enthusiasm as well.

Converting to trikes

Trikes are the simplest form of microlight, and for a hang-glider pilot with thirty hours or so in his logbook converting to a trike is not

Triking is fun. Light in weight, they climb well solo and need little space for take off and landing.

responsibility for knowing the controlled airspace regulations and other rules, such as relate to low flying (see p.159).

Schools and clubs which fly both hang gliders and microlights often run short conversion courses, and if the weather is good and you have the necessary experience you could be trike flying in a day. Then it pays to fly locally as much as you can so that you are really familiar with the trike's handling before flying cross-country.

Triking is probably the most sociable form of flying there is. Such slow, light aircraft can be landed on smooth hill tops, empty beaches, or farmers' fields (with permission), and enjoyable hours can be spent by a couple of pilots with two trikes exploring the countryside. A picnic lunch may be eaten on the moors, and small clouds chased on the way home! Such flying is not for the inexperienced but it is great to look forward to.

Cross-country flying demands many skills, e.g. an understanding of the weather; navigation, so you do not get lost; knowing how to make an emergency landing: and even using the terrain to your advantage.

You also need to know the laws concerning controlled airspace, since, unfortunately, it is not possible to wander through the sky as you please in this, or any other, country. Some airspace is reserved for air transport traffic, some for military use, for nuclear power plants, for gunnery ranges, and even for wild life. This does not leave too much for you but there is quite enough if you know where you may or may not fly.

To gain a pilot licence you have to pass exams on theoretical subjects, including air law, and you have to do them *before* the time comes when your instructor says this is a perfect day for your first cross-country.

Opposite: ½ million scale aeronautical chart.

The trike pilot can leave his engine and wheels on the ground and soar in the quiet sky with his friends.

122

11. Navigation: the basics

Flying along slowly above the open countryside and seeing the world spread out below you is a delightful way of spending a summer afternoon. There is so much to look at and the light and shadows are different each time you fly, even over the same route.

Navigation in a microlight is mainly by map reading, and this can be both enjoyable and accurate as long as you are familiar with maps and the information they present, and you give yourself plenty of practice. It is essentially a visual process, provided you can observe essential landmarks: if it is so hazy that you can only see for three miles you should stay close to your home field. Navigating must also be a readily adaptable process so that you can change your route, or even your destination, during the flight if the weather worsens.

The object in navigation is to avoid getting lost and blundering into controlled airspace, but it is almost as important that you do not spend so much time trying to find out where you are that you cannot pay enough attention to flying the aircraft properly. It is well known that a pilot who has lost himself is also likely to run out of petrol because his concentration is

elsewhere. The best way to avoid such ignominies is to think and learn about navigation before you start flying cross-country. Winter evenings and train journeys can be spent usefully, and pleasurably, studying maps to see where it would be fun to fly, and how to get there.

Something else you can usefully do ahead of time is to devise a means of reading your map in the air if you have no enclosed cabin to keep it from being blown away. A knee-pad holding a strip of map on rollers is a good idea, but it may limit your ability to fly in a different direction in order to circum-navigate bad weather. Study your microlight to get some ideas.

Maps and charts

The best maps for flying are the Topographical Air Charts obtainable from bookshops stocking H.M.S.O. publications, flying clubs and schools, and the Civil Aviation Authority. They present a great deal of information on surface features and are overprinted with controlled airspace details, such as control zones, airways, and special rules zones.

Study your microlight to find the best way to use your map without it blowing away. Here the pilot has fixed his map above his legs with rubber cords and can read it easily. He has orientated it with south towards the nose – the way he is going.

There are two topographical air charts in general use: the 1:500,000, or ½ million, series; and the 1:250,000, or ¼ million, series. The ½ million charts are very useful for planning and for obtaining controlled airspace information, but the scale is too small for most microlight pilots.

The larger scale 1:250,000 chart shows roads, large villages, and streams etc. in considerable detail, but controlled airspace only up to 3,000 ft. It is probably the most useful chart for microlight cross-country flying.

For local flying, and perhaps the first few short cross-country flights, the 1:50,000 (2 cm = 1km)

Ordnance Survey map can be very useful, particularly if the landscape has no prominent features. However, it does not contain any airspace information.

All charts give latitude and longitude. This is a useful means of locating small airstrips or for reporting a landing position. The latitude and longitude of any given point can be found from the scale along the side of the chart (latitude) and along the foot (longitude). The scale is divided into degrees and minutes (60 minutes to each degree; 1 minute = 1 nautical mile).

Any map used for flying should clearly show high ground and obstructions such as radio masts. Topographical Air Charts show high ground by layer tinting, the colours for each height band being printed somewhere near the edge of the chart.

Peaks which are noticeably higher than might be expected from the layer tint shown are marked by a spot height dot with the height above sea level printed alongside.

Obstructions of 300 ft or more above the ground are also clearly marked. However, there are many spires and chimneys lower than this which you might not see if you continue to fly in descending cloud.

Working out drift and ETA can be done without an office desk, provided you know how to make a good flight plan – and then carry it out.

Validity of map information

Although hills and the coastline stay much the same, the appearance of the land can be changed by new reservoirs or motorways, which may cause considerable confusion if they are not marked on the map. So check your maps from time to time against the updated ones at your local flying club, and if necessary buy new ones.

Orientation

Unless you are very experienced at map reading or orienteering it is easier to align your map so that your destination is ahead of the aircraft. All features and landmarks then turn up as anticipated to the left or right of the nose. If the map is held with north at the top, so that you can read all the place names, you may become confused, particularly if flying on a southerly course.

Reading the map

The first principles of practical map reading are to have, at any time, a known, identified, landmark in view, and not to lose sight of it until a further landmark in the intended flight direction has been positively identified. In other words: to know where you are all the time.

This does not mean identifying every village or minor road junction over which the aircraft passes. It is

¼ million scale

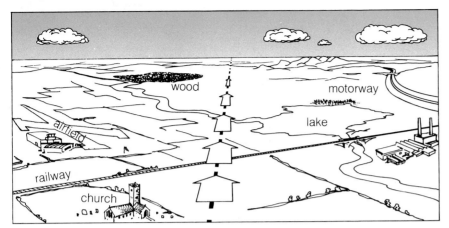

wood

motorway

lake

airfield

railway

church

It is not necessary to pass over the top of prominent landmarks when navigating by map, but to relate them to your position in the air.

not only unnecessary but wasteful of time and energy which could be better used for other things. It means being able to select important features and relate the position and heading of the aircraft to them so that you continue to fly the aircraft in the desired direction.

When identifying surface features you should study what you see on the ground and then locate them on the map, *not* look at a

feature or town on the map and try to find it on the ground.

The best way to practise map reading is to carry, or use, a map on every *local* flight. From one or two thousand feet above the take-off place study the *distant* countryside for prominent features, such as towns, headlands, steep ridges, and identify them on your map. Now draw a mental line to a distant feature to see which

landmarks you would fly over or pass on the way, and identify them. In this way you will develop a feel for map reading before it is necessary to put it to the test on your first cross-country. You will also quickly discover how haze and cloud shadows change the appearance of the landscape, as well as how towns can sometimes become invisibly hidden in shallow valleys.

Drift
If you point the nose of the aircraft towards a landmark some miles in the distance and fly towards it in a crosswind, you will discover that your actual path over the ground is like this.

The direction in which the nose

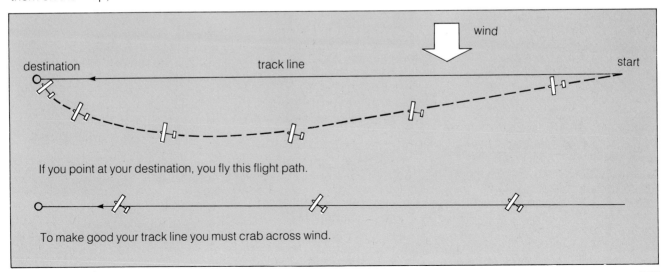

destination

track line

wind

start

If you point at your destination, you fly this flight path.

To make good your track line you must crab across wind.

If you fly low, navigation is more difficult because you see too much detail. From higher up you will see more prominent and unmistakable landmarks.

was pointing was not the direction in which you were actually going. If you want to fly straight along your track line to your destination in a crosswind you have to point the aircraft sufficiently into wind to balance the drift. This is called crabbing.

Experiment by flying a few kilometres along a straight road or canal which has the wind blowing across it. Failing to realise how the wind is drifting you away from where you want to go is a frequent preliminary to becoming lost.

If you are lost, or at least temporarily uncertain, the one thing not to do is to continue in

hope. You may be lucky and suddenly spot some well-known feature, but it is more likely that you become increasingly bewildered and cease to be able to recognise or identify anything at all. If you reach this stage you probably would not even recognise London airport if you found yourself over the top of it. So if you do not know where you are, stay within sight of a really prominent ground feature, such as a town with a railway line or a motorway junction, and do not leave it until, positively and honestly, you have identified it. Rigidly exclude wishful thinking; it does not work. When you have

identified your landmark do not leave it until you have also identified some related visible feature, so that you can then orientate yourself and set off once more in the correct direction.

If you cannot identify anything, choose a large field, land in it, and ask the farmer where you are. You will probably be unpopular, but this is better than blundering into controlled airspace.

Altitude
The height at which you fly and the visibility both have an appreciable effect on navigating by map. If you are flying at 1500–2000 ft the land seems to flatten out and significant hills and ridges may cease to be noticeable features. At the same time, however, a greater area of countryside is available for inspection. If you fly low, below 1000 ft, quite small undulations in the surface show up, but hills may obscure significant towns or lakes.

Flying low is often confusing because there is too much detail to look at: it literally is difficult to see the wood for the trees.

In very clear air the ground and its landmarks appear closer and more important than they actually are, while in hazy air both height and distances may seem greater than is actually the case.

Using your watch

Even before you start flying cross-country you should get into the habit of using your watch. Note the take-off time, time taken to climb to your chosen cruising height, time taken to fly between two landmarks where the distance is known, and landing time. A watch is a simple and readily available aid to map reading. You can check when some landmark is due to appear and what groundspeed is being achieved.

Using a compass

A compass enables you to fly in a straight line when visibility is poor, and between distant landmarks. On a microlight it should not be relied upon as a primary means of navigation as it is unlikely to be sufficiently accurate. For example, variation and deviation may not have been allowed for, or the compass may not be 'dead beat' enough, thus causing the card or needle to swing around, or it may not be mounted free from vibration.

The best way to use the compass is purely as an aid. Set off in the correct direction using landmarks and make any necessary correction for drift. When you have achieved the desired heading, check the compass reading. This can then be used to assist you to fly in a straight

line. You should re-check the compass from time to time using landmarks.

Variation

This is the difference between true geographical north and magnetic north, which is what the compass needle points towards. Variation varies from year to year and in different parts of the world, and is printed on aeronautical charts. At present in England it is 7° west of true north. This means that if you followed the compass without correction you would fly to the west, or left, of your intended direction. For the compass to

If you are lost do not wander about in hope. Fly around some good landmark and try to find where you are on the map. This castle is surrounded by open country in which you could land safely if necessary – the football field gives you a scale. Ahead there is a good-sized town. Study features such as railways, rivers or big roads and endeavour to identify it.

indicate the proper direction you must ADD the variation (7°) to the figure found by using a protractor on the map.

Deviation

A magnetic compass is affected by any magnetic substance close to it, such as a spanner or camera light

It is easy to get some precision into your navigation by this simple calculation.

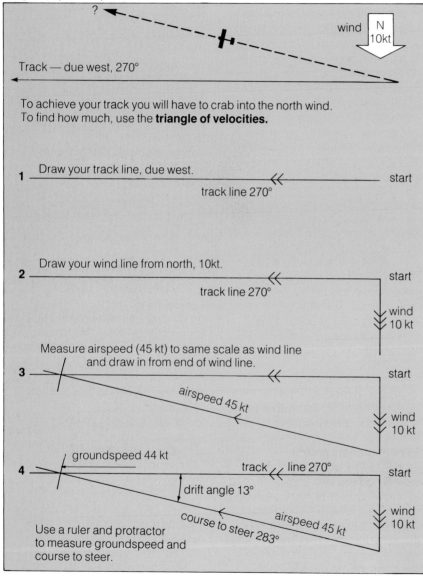

?

wind N 10kt

Track — due west, 270°

To achieve your track you will have to crab into the north wind.
To find how much, use the **triangle of velocities.**

1 Draw your track line, due west.

track line 270°

start

2 Draw your wind line from north, 10kt.

track line 270°

start

wind 10 kt

3 Measure airspeed (45 kt) to same scale as wind line and draw in from end of wind line.

airspeed 45 kt

start

wind 10 kt

4 groundspeed 44 kt

track line 270°

start

drift angle 13°

course to steer 283°

airspeed 45 kt

wind 10 kt

Use a ruler and protractor to measure groundspeed and course to steer.

meter, and the resulting deviation error may be considerable.

If the compass is fixed permanently in the aircraft the deviation for all headings can be found by pointing the aircraft in turn to north, south, east and west as determined by a separate hand-bearing compass well away from the aircraft, and by checking what the installed compass reads. You can then plot your compass deviation on a card so that you know what corrections to make in the air.

Make it a general rule to check that you have not put anything near the compass which could affect its accuracy.

Other errors
Compasses have other faults, such as dip and acceleration errors, which affect the rate at which the needle settles on to a new heading or steadies after a change in airspeed. For accuracy note the compass reading only when you are in steady flight.

Triangle of velocities

Your first cross-country flights may not last much above 40 minutes or take you more than 40 km from home, but as you gain experience you will want to range further and

Part of flight planning is to know whether you will get home before dark. Remember, it gets dark on the ground sooner than in the air.

discover new country. On longer flights the weather can change and the visibility worsen, so it is only sensible to make more precise calculations for drift than has been necessary so far.

This is done using the triangle of velocities, for which paper, protractor and ruler are needed. Imagine that you plan to fly to an airfield due W. (270°) of your base. The wind is N. (360°) at 10 knots and your cruise speed is 45 knots. To find out what heading (compass course) you should fly to counteract the wind, and what groundspeed you will achieve, you would plot your flight as follows:

1 Draw in your track line of 270° and mark with two arrows. It is best to make this line long; its exact length is immaterial.
2 Draw a line to represent the wind (360°, 10 knots). Use 10 units of any convenient size on your ruler to show 10 knots. Mark this line with 3 arrows. Remember, 'wind direction' means the direction *from* which the wind is coming. The arrows fly downwind.
3 With the ruler — or a pair of dividers — measure 45 knots using the same size units as for the 10-knot wind line, and draw a line from the end of the wind line so that it cuts the track line at 45 knots. Mark this line with one arrow. It is your course line.

4 With your protractor measure the heading you will need to fly to make good your track line, and with your ruler measure the length of the track line to obtain your groundspeed. This will be less than your airspeed of 45 knots.

Whenever you draw out a triangle of velocities always make a mental check to see whether the answer looks sensible, and that you have not done your plot from, for example, the wrong end of the wind line. In a crosswind your actual heading has to be to *windward* of your intended track.

When you have measured your groundspeed you will be in a position to work out how long the whole journey will take, e.g. if your destination is 60 nautical miles distant and your groundspeed is 40 knots, the flight should take 1 hour 30 minutes.

Finally, draw your track line on the map and mark on it the compass heading you will need to fly, and your groundspeed.

Units of measurement
Nautical miles and knots are established navigational units, and aeronautical charts carry a nautical mile scale. However, kilometres and km/h are just as satisfactory. Statute miles are least useful since many airspeed indicators are in knots and so it is easy to make an error. Avoid using a mixture of units.

Flight planning

It is worth planning a few flights before the great day arrives, so that you do not waste time getting yourself organised. The objectives of flight planning are to discover if your intended journey can be made:
a without infringing controlled airspace;
b without refuelling (will you need to land en route for petrol?);
c without meeting weather hazards which could have been foreseen;
d before night falls.
It will be to your advantage to take the following steps:
1 The first is to check on your map that your route is clear of control zones, etc. If the

straight line is not clear you will have to put in a turning point; so choose one which is prominent and unmistakable, even if it increases the distance to fly.

2   You know the speed at which your microlight cruises so work out how long it will take you, allowing for the wind expected at your flying height. Use the triangle of velocities.

3   Decide where you will refuel, if this is necessary.

4   Draw the final route on your map with a soft pencil and measure the distance accurately.

5   Double check that you have allowed enough margin for weather and for fuel; you should carry at least 40 per cent more fuel than you expect to use to reach your destination or next refuelling point.

6   It is helpful to mark the track line on the map with distances, say every 10 miles or kilometres.

   Now have a good look at your map and select landmarks and features which will be prominent from the air (your more local landmarks should already be familiar). These landmarks do not have to be on the track line; it is just as accurate to fly between, and equidistant from, for example, a hill and a reservoir. Check for radio

Cross-country check list

1. *Aircraft* Is it serviceable and ready to fly? Will tie-down pickets be needed?

2. *Pilot* Do you have enough warm clothes, a helmet, gloves, etc. AND money for making a phone call and the telephone number of your home airfield or instructor? Is your watch time correct?

3. *Navigation and weather*
   (i)   Does your map cover a large enough area outside your intended flight paths so that you could divert for fuel or bad weather if need be? Is the map up to date?
   (ii) Have you plotted your route correctly on the map and noted landmarks?
   (iii) Is your route clear of controlled airspace, high obstructions, difficult terrain? How long will the flight take?
   (iv) Is the weather suitable and unlikely to deteriorate during the estimated flight period — including possible time spent in refuelling or getting lost?
   (v)   Does your fuel tank hold enough for the flight plus 40% extra as a safety-margin?
   (vi) If not, how and where will you refuel? Is permission needed to land for refuelling?
   (vii) Can you complete the flight before dusk?
   (viii) Have you informed anyone of your plans, landing place and ETA?

masts or other obstructions near the route.

Setting off for the first time
To give yourself the best chance of success climb to your intended cruise height (e.g. 1,500 ft) close to your home field and set off on course from above the centre of the field, aiming for your first landmark. If, because of other traffic, this is not possible, your line

If you don't think there's time to fly home before nightfall, take your microlight by car.

should be drawn from a suitable departure point nearby. It is essential to start accurately.

When you depart allow for any crosswind and fly as straight as you can. As the first landmark gets nearer it should be obvious whether your allowance has been accurate. If you have not allowed enough — or even made too much allowance — adjust as necessary.

Unless you monitor your position continuously it is easy to become lost in a crosswind, because expected landmarks are increasingly seen from unexpected viewpoints. Headwinds and tailwinds are not as complicated, though a stronger tailwind than anticipated may result in your flying over strange country beyond your destination before you expect it, while an equally strong headwind may make your destination impossible to reach.

With practice the amount by which you should allow for a crosswind will become easier to judge. However, until you have made several successful cross-country flights you should be extra cautious about the wind strengths when flying. If your airspeed is only 40 knots a wind of 15 knots or more can have a devastating effect on your progress, particularly if it has any crosswind component.

12. Emergency landings

All the time you are flying keep a check on the wind direction. Movement of cloud shadows gives you wind direction at cloud height.

The three most likely reasons for a cross-country flight to come to a premature end are:

a engine failure, partial or total;
b deteriorating weather;
c losing your way.

Whatever the reason, you may have to land in a strange field and you may not have much time in which to work out what to do. So you need to be mentally prepared for something to go wrong at any time.

The first insurance against running out of both time and the chance of a good field is to fly at a height which will give some freedom of action — at least 1,000 ft over open country, and higher if the ground below has few fields. Many microlights have a good rate of climb, but without power the glide ratio is poor; on some no better than 1:8. This means that in calm air you can only glide a distance of 8,000 ft (2.4 km) from a height of 1,000 ft before arriving on the ground. In practice, the distance will actually be less because you have to allow plenty of height for your approach.

If there is a wind the distance you could fly into it will be less than 8,000 ft; although this will be more downwind, you will need some of it to turn into wind to land. In terms of thinking time you and your microlight will be on the ground from a height of 1,000 ft in less than three minutes from the engine becoming silent!

Although it is necessary to land into wind it is often difficult over open country to discover from which direction the wind is blowing. This is why you should keep a watch for wind direction indicators throughout the flight and not wait until you have an emergency to cope with. Wind direction information can be found from:

a the drift in relation to the track line;
b the wind direction in relation to the sun (if the flight is short the sun can be regarded as more or less stationary so you could say to yourself 'If my engine stops

If your engine stops at 1,000 ft you have only about 2.4 km (8,000 ft) in any direction in which to find a good field. If you fly at only 500 ft you may have a very small choice of landing places.

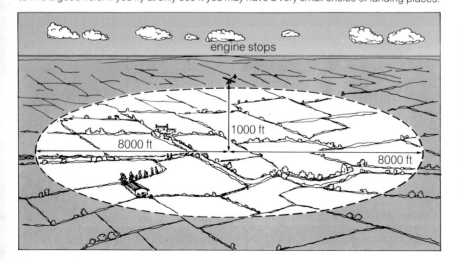

engine stops

1000 ft

8000 ft

8000 ft

Flying low across country gives you less chance of a good field if your engine stops. From this height you would have an enormous choice of fields. ▶

If you fly at this sort of height it is more difficult to assess fields, and you cannot see what is in valleys. ▼

For this pilot at this height there is no problem about an emergency landing field. There are plenty, and they are large.

Choose a field. The near field is large but contains sheep. Does it also have electric fences? What is growing in the other green fields and which way do they slope?

now I should go in to land with the sun off my left wingtip');

c smoke from chimneys, and steam from cooling towers;

d ripples running across standing crops or open water;

e movement of cloud shadows over the ground (this gives wind direction at cloud level: surface wind is usually a few degrees backed from cloud level wind);

f windsocks, windmills, and your own drift (this should be very noticeable if you are not flying very high).

Unreliable indicators are washing on lines or any other similar indicators near to buildings, hills, gullies, etc.

Choosing the field

Although the actual technique for landing will differ according to whether some power is available, the first priority is to choose a good, large field within easy reach. The best one may even be directly below but unseen because you are busy looking at more distant meadows. Choose your field on the basis of *size, slope* and *surface* in that order.

Size

The field should be as large as possible. It is better to land in the middle of an enormous field and have a long walk, than to cartwheel into a tiny one which is next to a pub and telephone. The field can be relatively narrow provided the length is into wind.

Try to assess the actual *size* of the field in relation to something else, such as a churchyard or motorway, since if all the fields in the area are very small, a bigger one may look deceptively large.

Size, of course, means landable area, which is reduced by surrounding obstructions, such as high trees and power wires, at the approach end. Obstructions at the upwind end of the field where you should have finished your landing run are unimportant — except for the turbulence they produce in a strong wind.

Telephone wires and low-voltage power wires (11,000 volts) often lie along roadside hedges and are difficult to see. Allow extra height when coming in, just in case.

Slope

Landing down a slope is not as important for a microlight as it is for a glider, where any downslope at all means ending up in the far hedge. Nevertheless, a downslope will add appreciably to your landing run.

If the ground slopes down more than 1 in 10 you will not stop. Of course it is possible to swing round or ground-loop to avoid colliding with the end of the field, but this always risks damage to the aircraft — and perhaps to you. It is always better, therefore, if you can land on level ground or on a slight up-slope.

Sometimes you may be faced with the alternative of landing into wind and downhill, or downwind and up the slope. For a slow microlight landing into wind is always preferable and safer. If you only discover that your field slopes steeply at the last moment you are an incompetent observer. Assessing slope in local fields from the air — and checking on foot to see if you were correct — is something you can practise long before you make your first cross-country.

Indications of field slope include:

a the way it lies in relation to other fields and the horizon;

b the way it relates to canal and railway cuttings and embankments;

c grass and crops are usually darker and more lush at the lower end, and gateways muddier;

d fields normally slope down towards streams, rivers, and natural lakes (not reservoirs).

Surface

Rough surfaces and standing crops damage aircraft, and wrecked crops infuriate farmers.

Good surfaces include:

a new pasture (old pasture can be tussocky);

b harrowed and prepared soil;

c very small seedling crops — provided you land along the rows and keep spectators OUT of the field.

Bad surfaces include:

a vegetable crops, such as kale, rape and broccoli;

b standing corn or hay;

c fields covered with baled straw;

d ploughed fields, particularly if boggy or frozen.

Animals should be considered under this heading, especially if they are spread evenly over the field. In general sheep tend to huddle together, but may suddenly bolt as a mass. Cattle are usually slower to move, but may be remarkably curious after the aircraft has landed and come to eat it! Horses are least reliable and may gallop about nervously in any direction.

If there is no reasonable alternative to landing in a field with animals, avoid frightening them on the approach, and touch down as far away from them as possible. After landing stay with the aircraft and endeavour to move it to the gate, or to a suitable sheltered corner of the field. Do not let animals escape with you through the gate.

The approach

Having selected a good field you now have to get down safely into it. You may have to do this by gliding if your engine has stopped, or it may be possible to use power to adjust your approach path. This is usually the case if you are landing because of deteriorating weather, or because you are lost and becoming short of fuel.

If you do have power available, land while you still have it. There is no sense in flying around lost until the engine finally runs out of petrol and doubles your problem. Use it to inspect the field and make a good approach, but do not rely on the engine continuing to run.

Obviously, if your engine splutters or stops you should make an effort to find the cause and get it going again, but only if you have enough spare height *and* you are in easy reach of good fields. If you are lost and fuel is low in the tank, it may suck out water or other debris (which should not be there, but sometimes is). If you are landing because of low cloud, drizzle, or snow, the air will be moist and cold and you could have ice forming in the air intake or carburettor to cause loss of power.

Never try to restart if you are getting so low that you will have no time to plan and execute a safe landing. For example, if you lose power at 2,000 ft you could allow

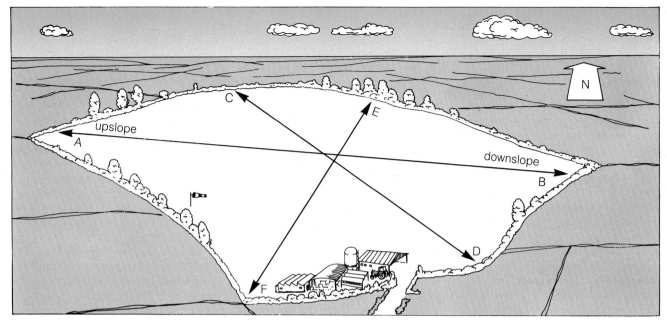

yourself to work on getting the engine going again until you are down to 1,500 ft, or perhaps 1,200 ft. Below this, forget about the engine, switch off the ignition and fuel, and concentrate entirely on your field and how you are going to approach and land in it safely.

If the engine has failed at such a low height that there is no time to do anything except just get down into any clear space ahead, CLOSE the throttle fully. There is nothing worse when trying to pull off a difficult emergency landing than to have your engine suddenly surge into life with full power. It could be fatal.

Without your engine your microlight is a glider, and the principle of landing a glider in the right place is to fly a path of a length which will use up the height between the aircraft and the

ground exactly — no more, no less. This demands good judgement; it helps to fly a pattern which is adjustable as this gives the best chance of success. Remember, the altimeter does not give you the height above the field.

When you have decided on your field and discovered the wind direction:

a If you have plenty of height to spare, fly around it so you can look at it from different directions. This may show up slope, or an unexpected rock or obstruction which would have been invisible from the straight-in approach line.

b If you have no spare height — or when you are ready to make your approach — fly to a point upwind and to one side of the field, and then turn downwind (you are now on a normal circuit

Assessing a field. The run A–B is the longest, but it slopes uphill to the west which reduces its effective length. Run C–D is shorter, though flatter and has no serious obstructions at either end. Run E–F is very short with tall obstructions at the north end, which probably makes it useless. Taking off to the south might give enough length but it passes close to the buildings. This might be unacceptable to the farmer.

downwind leg except that your field may be much smaller than your usual airfield). If you are short of height join the down-wind leg part way along it.

Look at your field and visualise where you should turn on to base leg, and where you would turn into wind for your final approach. If you find yourself high slightly edge a little further out from the field to lengthen your flight path; if you are low, keep close, but do not crowd

What is growing in the two nearest fields? How much does the field with the sheep slope? Could you reach the large harrowed fields beyond the wood?

This microlight pilot is not very high, which field should he go for?

◀ What choices do you have? Which way is the wind blowing?

◀ Problems. That lovely engine goes all quiet. What do you do? What turbulence would you expect near the ground?

There are a few small landing places. Could you reach them from this height?

yourself so that you are forced to turn into wind from a 180° turn. A crosswind base leg of some length is necessary to allow you to judge the best moment for turning on to finals.

Continue with your assessment — 'am I too high', 'am I getting low?' — and make small adjustments accordingly. Keep checking your airspeed. Is it sufficient for a power-off approach and to cope with wind gradient? If you are lower than you would like to be get the nose down to *increase* speed. It is a common fault to hold the nose up unconsciously when under-shooting, and it only results in your coming down faster, or even stalling.

Remember, if on finals you find yourself drifting sideways, because you are out of wind, lower the *into-wind* wing immediately: not too much, but enough to cause the aircraft to slip sideways into wind. If you are almost on the ground, and so do not have enough height to do this, put on *downwind* rudder just before touchdown to swing the nose in the same direction as the drift.

After *any* field landing you must contact the farmer, or person under whose authority the field comes, without delay. If you have caused damage to the field or its contents you or your insurance company should pay for it.

As with so many things in flying, you need to take decisions in time. Avoid dithering or wandering aimlessly around in the vague hope that something will turn up. Take decisions, if possible, while there is still time to assess their value. If there is no time, stick to the decision you have already made.

Flying from a farmer's field
It is more fun to fly your microlight from a country field than from an airport, but if you have the chance to use a farm field you will need to check its suitability. It is not just a matter of landing, but, more importantly, of taking off safely.

You need to know the length of your own aircraft's take-off run in windless conditions on a level grass surface, and your rate of climb. These you can measure when flying from your usual airfield. Let us say your take-off is normally 75 metres and your rate of climb 500 ft per minute.

Now measure the length of your chosen field in all the directions in which a safe take-off could be made, and assess the height of obstructions at the upwind end of each run. Plot your aircraft performance against the field dimensions. With no wind you should be able to clear any obstructions by *at least* 50 ft.

If there is a wind you will, of course, have more than 50 ft over

the obstructions, but on a hot, windless day you will have less. If the grass is long or the ground soft or muddy, or covered with a thin layer of slushy snow, you may not even get off the ground before the far hedge comes too close for comfort. So do not think that just because microlights leap quickly into the air any field will do, however willing the farmer is to let you use it. If you have a choice, go for the largest, smoothest field there is. It should also be fairly level, otherwise taking off uphill may be difficult except in a fresh wind.

Never fly from a field without one or more windsocks or plastic streamers, and NEVER FLY ALONE, or at least without telling some reliable friend of your plans in detail.

13. Weather

Microlights are weather-sensitive aircraft and most are unsuitable for flying in strong or gusty winds, thermal or other turbulence, or in freezing rain or fog. So you need to understand something about the weather: what causes cloud to descend to the ground, how to recognise what is happening from the clouds you can see, and how to extract the maximum information from newspaper or television weather maps. If you know how to read the clouds, they will tell you all you want to know about the weather for the next 4–5 hours and for a distance of up to about 40 miles.

This chapter provides only a small amount of information about a very large subject and more specialised books should be studied if you are serious about your flying.

Pressure

Apart from the sun itself, the dominant factor in producing weather is the pressure of the air. All over the world the standard pressure at sea level (at 15°C) is 1013.25 millibars. In a deep depression, or *low*, the surface pressure may descend to a little less than 960 mb, while in a big anticyclone, or *high*, it may rise above 1040 mb.

The practical effects of rising or falling pressure are to vary the strength and direction of the wind, and the amount of cloud. When pressure falls the air is generally rising, expanding and cooling over a large area. When it is rising the air is generally descending, compressing and warming. These processes directly affect the amount of cloud that develops.

With increasing altitude the air pressure falls relative to the surface pressure. At 18,000 ft the pressure is only about 500 mb. (In water the pressure increases by 500 mb only 17 ft (5 metres) below the surface!)

Temperature

Temperature falls with increasing height, in a predictable manner; the rate of temperature change is termed the *lapse rate*. If the air is dry (clear of cloud) it falls at 3C° per 1,000 ft, and when it is saturated (as in cloud or fog), at 1.5C° per 1,000 ft. However, this process can be locally or temporarily affected by other factors. Strong anticyclonic subsidence, for example, will put an effective lid on the lapse rate, producing a layer of air in which the temperature ceases to fall, or may even rise slightly. This is called an *inversion*. Massive thunderstorm development will also affect the lapse rate,

In clear air the temperature falls with height at 3C° per 1,000 ft (the dry adiabatic lapse rate). In cloud air cools at only 1.5C° per 1,000 ft (the saturated adiabatic lapse rate). The act of condensation of water vapour into cloud liberates heat, so the strength of the thermal will increase inside an active cumulus.

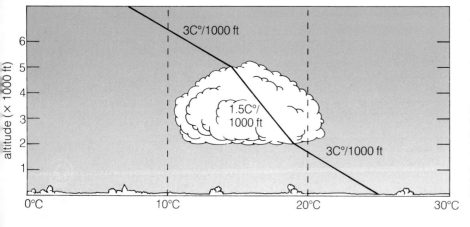

A deep depression over Iceland. The steep pressure gradient between the high and the low is giving very strong winds, as is seen from the close spacing of the isobars. This squeeze sometimes occurs between an Atlantic low and a big anticyclone over NE Europe which can bring strong, cold northern winds over the whole of Britain.

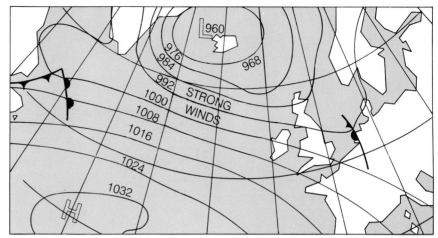

particularly when storms, having carried huge quantities of warmer air to great heights, are collapsing.

Wind

Wind is air moving from higher to lower pressure, although it does not flow directly from an anti-cyclone towards a depression because the rotation of the earth causes a circulatory flow around these pressure systems (see diagrams). Depressions approaching over the British Isles usually develop far out in the Atlantic from a meeting of cold polar air from the north and warmer moist air from nearer the equator. Due to the earth's rotation, these warm and cold 'fronts' swing round each other and a new depression is born. Their passage towards Northern Europe, and their eventual decay, can be followed from daily weather maps.

Since there cannot only be areas of lower than mean pressure, anticyclones develop. These high pressure areas sometimes establish themselves so strongly that they divert oncoming lows, or slow them in their tracks. When this happens the wind is squeezed between the two systems and becomes very strong.

Cloud

As air rises, expands and cools it becomes less able to carry moisture as invisible water vapour. As cooling continues, some of this invisible water vapour condenses to form cloud or fog. This is what

In the northern hemisphere

the circulation around a low is anti-clockwise; around a high it is clockwise.

Flying towards a warm front. This sectional view shows conditions relatively near to the front itself. The early warning from high cirrus can be observed while the front is perhaps 150 miles distant.

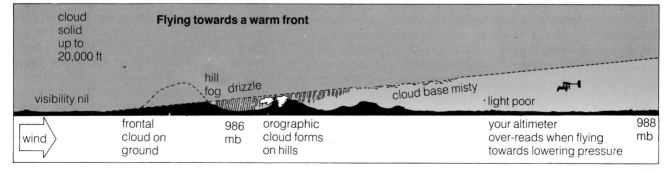

Flying towards a warm front

cloud solid up to 20,000 ft

visibility nil

hill fog   drizzle

cloud base misty

· light poor

| wind | frontal cloud on ground | 986 mb | orographic cloud forms on hills | your altimeter over-reads when flying towards lowering pressure | 988 mb |

Never get trapped in valleys with cloud on the hills. Turn back before it happens.

In such weather orographic cloud may form below the cloud cover and join up with it leaving you like the ham in the sandwich.

After the front passes, cloud will lessen or thin to some extent. Try to see if there is high cloud above the ragged cloudlets or whether the sky is clear.

happens when a depression develops: air is slowly lifted, and as it cools it produces increasing quantities of cloud. The air ahead of the warm front flows up gently over cooler air and is cooled by this, as well as by rising. Cloud forms at great heights well ahead of the front, and steadily lowers towards the front, where it may be on the ground. This produces hill fog and drizzle.

The following cold front, where cold air is undercutting warmer air ahead and pushing it up, produces squall clouds and heavier rain. If the fronts *occlude*, i.e. the cold front overtakes the warm front, rain will be both drizzly and made up of

If the sky clears rapidly after a cold front there may be plenty of blue sky but the wind may also quickly become very strong.

larger droplets.

When air subsides, as it does in an anticyclone, there is a warming and drying effect so cloud will lessen or may even evaporate altogether. The subsidence of the air does, however, concentrate dust particles, which means visibility will deteriorate. At night, radiation cooling into a cloudless sky is what produces fog over low ground.

This is obviously an over-simplification of a very complex process, but it contains a fundamental piece of information useful to know when you are flying: when pressure begins to fall an increase in cloud cover should be expected or, in other words, when cloud cover is thickening and lowering, pressure is falling.

1016 | H | 1016 | 1000 1008 | 1016 | 1024 | H

Trailing front. Approaching low pressure is being affected by the high, causing the front to slow down and trail, and re-develop as a warm front in some places and a cold front in others. Small new wave depressions, or secondaries, tend to form on such trailing fronts, which are sometimes both fierce and fast moving.

On days with some wind, cumulus clouds may form in 'streets'. There may be lift underneath them or down-currents in between. Try to find where the air is smoothest and fly along this line parallel to the cloud streets.

The weather map

Properly called a synoptic chart, the weather map presents pressure patterns at the earth's surface and the associated weather. To obtain the most value from a forecast you need to be able to interpret the information it gives you. Charts are also produced for about 18,000 ft and 30,000 ft altitude for the meteorologist to use when making his forecast, but these are not so readily available.

Pressure is plotted on the chart with lines joining places of equal pressure. The lines are called *isobars*, and they are usually spaced 4 or 8 mb apart, depending on the scale of the chart. Where the isobars are close together, this shows a steep pressure gradient — and strong winds. Where isobars are far apart the gradient is slack and the winds light.

In the northern hemisphere the circulation around a depression is anticlockwise, while around a high

Cumulus clouds have flat bases, which is most marked when you are flying near cloudbase.

Watch cumulus to see if they are visibly producing towering heads. If they are the air underneath the cloud will be rough and turbulent.

A day with plenty of active cumulus and probably quite a lot of turbulence. If you do not like it rough, wait until the late afternoon when thermals become more widely spaced and the air begins to quieten down.

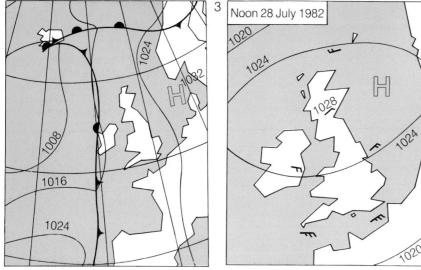

3
Noon 28 July 1982

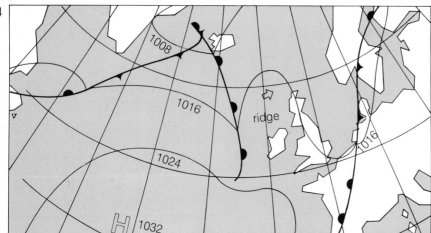

A ridge of high pressure often gives a single fine day between depressions. As the ridge passes through, the wind first veers and slackens, and later backs and freshens; the amount of cloud increases.

A large established anticyclone may hold a front stationary for several days; and it could be raining underneath for just as long.

Anticyclone. The wind is slackest in the centre of a high where the pressure is also highest, but it will be strong along the English Channel as it funnels from the NE between England and France. The temperature is lower on windward coasts than where the air has had time to warm up passing over the land.

height. As air heated by the warm ground rises, it cools, and when the cooling air in a thermal reaches its dew point, condensation takes place and a cumulus cloud develops. You will notice on a summer morning that cumulus develop at much the same height all over the sky (condensation level). Such cumulus have a short life of about 15–20 minutes, so that at any given moment about half the cumulus in the sky are growing and the other half decaying. Cloud base is lowest in the morning and rises during the day, in Britain reaching 3,000–6,000 ft, depending on the temperature and the amount of moisture in the air. In the late afternoon thermals become more widely separated, and the air in them becomes less rough. Cumulus evaporate and disappear during early evening. In northern Europe thermals strong enough to be of use to glider pilots begin to develop in early March, may be at their best in June, and die away in October.

Apart from producing rising air which a pilot can use, cumulus clouds tell you a great deal about what is happening to the weather. If they disappear in early afternoon

it is clockwise. Charts 1–4 show typical weather patterns from which a wide variety of weather can be deduced — different in summer and winter, and some of it perfect for microlight flying. Occurring within these larger patterns, in certain conditions, is

another very important factor: small-scale convection, or thermals.

Convection
Thermals, and the cumulus clouds they produce, will only develop when the temperature falls with

it could be because pressure is rising as an anticyclone intensifies; or is it because the air has become stable as the high cloud moves in ahead of an approaching warm front? If cumulus grow large and tall during the morning, this could indicate thunderstorms for the afternoon; if they grow large but flat, thereby covering the sky, this is an indication that the air is very moist and unsettled weather may not be too far away.

You should keep clear of big cumulus and cumulo-nimbus (thunderhead) clouds since, apart from strong up-currents, the air underneath them may be extremely turbulent. Heavy rain or hail can start to fall quite suddenly, and if the air is hazy you may not observe what is happening until too late. Be warned.

Seabreezes

On a day with strong convection currents the masses of rising air over the hot land pull in cool air from the sea. This can bring a large and sudden change in wind direction, so that you could find yourself landing downwind even though you had taken off into wind

time of day

The cloudbase rises during the day

altitude (ft)

—5000

—3000

—1000

CONDENSATION LEVEL

small cumulus in morning

largest cumulus at time of maximum heating

cumulus die away in late afternoon

08.00 10.00 12.00 14.00 16.00 18.00

30,000 ft

anvil cloud   hail grows

pileus

cu-nb

mammatus cloud

wind

down draught

cold heavy rain or hail

air rising into cloud

cool air

squall wind

calm before storm

The calm before the storm is due to the air rising to feed the cu-nb (cumulo-nimbus) and effectively cancelling the wind. It is followed by squalls and gusts blowing out from the cold air downfall. This is when microlights blow away.

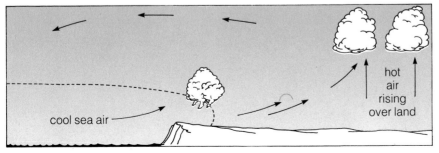

cool sea air

hot air rising over land

Cool sea air is pulled in by masses of warmed air, which is rising over the land. Even when it has moved in ten miles or so there may still be little or no cloud forming in the sea air, so it can provide smooth and pleasant flying.

in that direction only a few minutes earlier. The sea air along the coast, which is clear of cumulus clouds, is smoother and visibility is often better; if you are tired of being bounced around in your microlight in the thermals, fly along the coast in the sea air.

If the sea breeze and the main prevailing wind converge a line of

If the air is dry cloudbase will be higher; if the air is anticyclonic clouds will remain small, and the air below them somewhat hazy.

If the air is moist cloudbase will be low, but visibility on such days is usually good.

Late in the afternoon on a day of good cumulus development the clouds often become slightly tinged with colour, usually due to the larger droplets which make up each cloud. There is no threat in these clouds — they are beginning to die away.

Weather check list

Before you fly:

1 Obtain the latest forecast and study it in relation to the route you plan to fly. (E.g. are you flying towards an approaching warm front?)

2 Consider wind strength and gustiness. (E.g. is a pressure squeeze likely to produce stronger winds than expected; does your course lie to the lee of hills; is convection likely to be strong with thermals rough?)

3 Will visibility be good enough? (E.g. in anticyclonic haze visibility will worsen downwind of large towns.)

4 If thunderstorms are forecast, can you complete the flight before they develop to a troublesome extent?

5 If rain is forecast, is it likely to be accompanied by low orographic cloud in hilly areas on your route; or is the air ahead of the rain sufficiently cold for it to turn to snow? (Remember that, whereas flying in rain may be unpleasant, if it suddenly becomes snow you will not be able to see anything.)

6 If it becomes necessary to divert around squalls, can this be done safely and over open country?

7 If you are going to return to a coastal field is it likely by the time you return that:
 a a sea breeze will have come in and the wind have changed;
 b sea fog could have developed and drifted in over the coast?

quite large cumulus may develop along the meeting zone. It is recognisable because cloud base is usually lower than the cumulus inland, and there may be little rags of cloud hanging underneath. Up-currents may be found underneath the cloud line.

During the afternoon the sea breeze tends to move slowly inland, perhaps 20 miles or so, before dying away in the late afternoon or early evening.

Micromet and local weather

It will not take you long to discover that locally the weather can be quite different from what could be expected from the general forecast. Sea breezes are an example.

Flying a light, slow microlight in hilly country will be very different from wandering about over a flat plain. Not only does the wind

Airflow over and around mountains can be violent and unpredictable if the wind is strong. Wave lift may be smooth, but you may have an unacceptably rough ride trying to find it.

cease to blow in a smooth and ordered manner, but it can set up wave systems of extraordinary power, reaching great heights. All this can be studied in books, but there is no substitute for learning from your own observations and from other pilots' experience of wind and weather differences in your locality. Until you have, do not fly your microlight among hills, near cliffs, or along valleys under low cloud.

Using the terrain

Any light, slow, and low-powered aircraft is affected to an appreciable extent by the ups and downs of the air, caused by thermal up-currents and the sink between them, wind flowing up over the face of hills and the curl-over in their lee. Careful observation of how the air behaves will not only enable you to fly more smoothly, but it can also save you fuel. Remember, a microlight is a very weather-sensitive aircraft.

To make the best use of the

Top: If the air is very unstable clouds grow fast and tall; if it is also moist, squalls form readily with cloudbase often lower than expected. The air under, and in the vicinity of, such clouds can be extremely turbulent, and the squalls move quickly.

Below: Clouds of a smooth elliptical shape, or in bars like these, are signs of atmospheric waves, usually set up to the lee of mountains. If you are in the upgoing part of the wave the air may be smooth, but elsewhere it can be very rough with strong down-draughts and rotors.

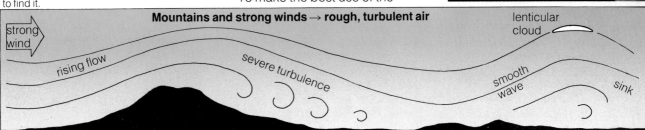

Mountains and strong winds → rough, turbulent air

strong wind

rising flow

severe turbulence

smooth wave

lenticular cloud

sink

The Beaufort Scale

Symbol	Force	Description	Effects	Wind kt	Windsock
⊙	0	Calm	Smoke rises vertically.	1	
	1	Light air	Wind shows smoke drift; may not disturb windsock.	1 – 3	
	2	Light breeze	Wind felt on face. Leaves rustle.	4 – 6	
	3	Gentle breeze	Leaves in constant motion. Flags lift.	7 – 10	
	4	Moderate wind	Dust swirls. Small branches move.	11 – 15	
	5	Fresh wind	Small trees sway. Microlights blow over.	16 – 21	
	6	Strong wind	Large branches sway. Umbrellas uncontrollable.	22 – 27	
	7	Moderate gale	Difficulty walking against wind.	28 – 33	
	8	Gale	Twigs break off trees.	34 – 40	
	9	Strong gale	Chimney pots take off.	41 – 47	
	10	Whole gale	Trees take off.	48 – 55	

Gale warnings are issued if the wind is expected to increase to force 8 or gusts of 43 knots or more are expected. The word *imminent* means within 6 hours, *soon* means 6 – 12 hours and *later* means more than 12 hours.

Visibility

Good	More than 5 nautical miles
Moderate	2 – 5 nautical miles
Poor	900 metres – 2 nautical miles
Mist/ haze	1000 metres – 2000 metres
Fog	Less than 1000 metres at sea or 700 metres on land
Dense fog	Less than 20 metres

Fronts

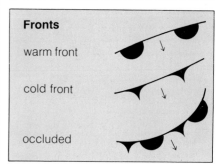

warm front

cold front

occluded

terrain over which you fly you need to start thinking about it when you plan your route. Look at the map for ridges and lines of hills near your track line. If you alter your line slightly so that you fly along the windward side you will be in any rising air there is. If you stay on the lee side you will be in downgoing and probably turbulent air, and you will use more fuel. If you plan to fly along coastal cliffs over the beach and the prevailing wind is blowing from the land, you will be in or near the turbulent air which is curling over the cliffs; if a seabreeze develops, the air will start to rise over the cliffs, even though it is still

blowing from the opposite direction inland.

Using thermals to save fuel — or to enjoy yourself — is practicable on many microlights. You can leave the engine running at reduced power while you circle up in the lift, and then fly on course again at whatever power setting you decide you need. If cumulus are lying in streets, find the line of lift and fly along it. The upcurrent will not be continuous but probably frequent enough to help you on your way. Make sure you are not sucked into cloud: if you are gaining height faster than you expected, keep looking up, and if

the cloud seems close and wispy, fly away from the street into downgoing air.

Thermals are bred from sunshine, so you will find more buoyant rising air over sunlit land than areas covered in shadow.

Finding out how to take advantage of the terrain and thermals is good for your flying. It will make you a more observant pilot and help you fly more accurately. Should you one day have engine failure, it could help you stay longer in the air and so have a better choice of emergency landing fields — even if it does not enable you to get all the way home.

14. Flying on floats

Some microlights have been designed so that the landing wheels can be easily and quickly exchanged for skis (to enable you to fly off packed snow or ice), or for floats. There are also amphibians, having wheels which can be raised or lowered to allow flying from both land and water. Some parts of the world, such as Canada with its thousands of lakes, are ideal for float flying.

Floats are made from foam covered with a thin glass-fibre skin, or from thin plywood, aluminium sheet, or materials like carbon fibre and kevlar. Most floats weigh about 25–30 kg a pair, though the weight can be reduced to 14 kg when they are made of more expensive materials. Even this low weight, plus the extra drag, is greater than a pair of wheels and:

a may increase the aircraft's weight to more than that allowed for a microlight;

b will reduce your rate of climb;

c will increase your sink rate when gliding in to land, and

d will slightly increase your stall speed.

The Eagle has had its main wheels exchanged for floats, but there is no need to remove the nose wheel, which will be clear of the water. Note the position of the step on the bottom of the floats.

Floats may also alter the c.g. (centre of gravity) of the aircraft, and this must be checked BEFORE you fly.

In the air the large mass of the floats, compared with wheels, will probably give your aircraft a more ponderous feel, particularly in pitch, so be prepared for this. If you are used to side-slipping your

microlight when approaching to land, be careful; you may find that:

a speed increases more than you expect, and

b recovery is slower.

Some floats have water rudders, usually connected to the ordinary rudder pedals. They are needed to steer the aircraft when taxiing and to help keep a straight path when taking off and landing. If your aircraft is an amphibian the water

rudders may have to be retractable for when you land on the wheels. Remember to lower them before landing on water otherwise you may have no control over where you go.

Microlights are more weather-sensitive on water than on land, and you should not attempt to take off if the wind is more than 10–12 knots, or the waves are more than 15 cm high — and then only if you have some experience.

Taxiing

If there is any wind you will find that the aircraft's tendency to weathercock into wind is also greater on water than on land where the wheels have at least some grip on the surface. It can sometimes be very difficult indeed to turn downwind to taxi to your take-off position; if the wind is up to 10 knots you may not be able to turn out of wind at all, and merely skitter over the surface going backwards. It may be simpler to tow your aircraft to the take-off place with a boat.

Left: Formation take-off. Note how the Eagle is almost up on the step while the Mirage is still endeavouring to accelerate.

Right: Clear of the water and climbing away.

Taking off

Your take-off run on water will be appreciably longer than from land — perhaps more than five times if there is no wind — so allow plenty of space ahead.

Apart from endeavouring to keep straight, the problem with floats is to get them to unstick from the water. The bottoms of floats are stepped, having an abrupt change

What happens if height is misjudged on the landing? It is difficult to get the microlight out of the water without causing it further damage. Night could well fall first.

in the underwater shape at about a half to two-thirds of the way back: when stationary the aircraft may sit with the full length of the floats in contact with the water, or the floats may assume this position as you start to accelerate. Your objective is to get 'up on the step' so that only the front section of each float is in the water; the aircraft will then accelerate enough to reach flying speed and lift off the water.

The difficulty, as you open the throttle and start to accelerate, is that the drag of the floats in the water is greater than that of the rest of the aircraft in the air, which tends to nose over, causing the floats to dig in. It is essential to do all you can to keep the nose up — this means holding the stick back. Then, as you come up on the step you must move the stick forwards to allow the aircraft to accelerate. When you are reaching flying speed apply increasing back pressure to overcome the suck of the floats, and get airborne. It is all fairly critical, and a matter of getting the attitude right within one

Top: It is better to have a slight ruffling of the surface, so that height can be easily assessed

Below: The water surface is still ruffled but the breeze is dying — the water could become glassy quite quickly, and make it difficult to know how high you are.

Top: It is better to have a slight ruffling of the surface, so that height can be easily assessed

or two degrees at crucial stages of take-off. Every effort must be made to avoid trying to take off nose low; if the floats drop back into the water the sudden increase in drag may start the aircraft porpoising, which can quickly get out of hand. Once clear of the water check your airspeed before climbing away.

Landing

Approach as usual into wind, and try to hold off until the aircraft subsides onto the water. Be prepared for airspeed to fall off more quickly than with wheels, and for a more rapid deceleration after touchdown. Do not fly onto the water as this increases the risk of the floats digging into waves.

Landings are easier when there are small ripples on the water to disturb the surface. If the water is so calm and smooth that it reflects the sky it will be impossible to land on it in the normal way. You will suddenly discover that you cannot judge if you are 5 feet up or 50.

Glassy water landings

Apart from landing close to the shore to obtain some reference there are only two ways to overcome this situation:

a have someone in a small boat disturb the water surface when you want to come in and land, or

b make a powered approach at a relatively slow speed so that the

Below: The water surface is still ruffled but the breeze is dying — the water could become glassy quite quickly, and make it difficult to know how high you are.

aircraft will be in landing attitude when it reaches the surface you cannot see.

This is standard practice for aeroplanes which approach at an established power setting/airspeed relationship, and is possible because they are suitably instrumented: few microlights have the equipment. The glassy water landing technique can, of course, be used at night, provided the water is known to be clear of obstructions, and sometimes in the snow condition known as *whiteout*, when it is impossible to

Pterodactyl on floats. How high are you flying – 2 metres or 200, or are you actually sitting on the surface?

distinguish the sky from the surface.

Rough water landings

Landings — or take-offs — with surface waves more than 15 cm high will probably result in damage, since:

a you may be bounced back into the air, or

b the aircraft may dig in or break a float: the water is very hard when you hit it at 25–30 knots.

On the sea the surface wavelets may be very small, but with a bigger and longer swell resulting from an old storm a long distance away, or even a large ship. This swell will probably not lie in the same direction as the wind, and so you have to make your choice of landing either into wind and across the swell, or out of wind and along the swell. If the wind is more than 2–3 knots you must land into it — which immediately limits the safe height and wavelength of the swell in which you can operate. If there is almost no wind, land along the rising side of the swell crest. If the swell is slight, but is coming in through water which shallows gradually as it nears the shore, this will steepen the swell, perhaps to the extent of breaking crests.

If you are in doubt about the roughness of the sea or the size of the swell it may be safer to land your float-plane on land. If you

choose a smooth grass field — better if wet — or a flat and empty sandy beach, and land carefully, you will probably do little damage, perhaps none at all. It will almost certainly be less than the battering your aircraft would receive in rough water.

Leaving a microlight on the water

In a country, such as Britain, where wind and weather changes are frequent, a light float-plane moored out on the water is very vulnerable. On an airfield, if the wind starts gusting, it takes little time to tie down a microlight securely, or to put it in a hangar. But if you cannot get to your microlight except by dinghy it is likely to have blown over long before you reach it. If it capsizes and fills with water it will be extremely difficult to rescue since the weight of the water will distort or perhaps break the structure (you may also be left with corrosion problems to deal with).

When moored from the floats the aircraft will keep heading into wind

as this fluctuates in direction; on a lake or reservoir it should be safe in a very light wind. On the sea, the tide creates difficulties since it may flow in a different direction from the wind, and become strong enough to turn the aircraft out of wind. If your microlight is moored among boats remember that the latter will be affected by the tide changing much more than will the aircraft, mainly because their hulls are deeply submerged while the aircraft's floats just rest on the surface: it could mean that the large clear space you thought your aircraft was in has disappeared!

The tidal flow will, of course, sweep an aircraft along while it is taxiing, and almost certainly in a direction in which the pilot does not wish to go. At high and low tide there are periods of slack water, which make operations easier, but it is altogether better to operate from a lake or reservoir if this is at all possible.

Always carry a light heaving line on the aircraft, perhaps with a small hook or anchor at the end. It

Without anchor and in a tideway or a wind a shore handling party is a help. Stop the engine before you start climbing about on the floats.

may one day prevent you drifting or being swept away if your engine stops — although a trike can be sailed downwind if the control bar is pushed fully out. It is probably altogether safer to lift your microlight out of the water and tie it down on the shore.

Equipment and safety

If your float-flying is to be local you will need only some form of protection for yourself: either a wet suit, or one of the many lifejackets or buoyancy aids on the market — or both. If, however, you intend flying over longer stretches of water it is only sensible to:

a inform the coastguard of your route and ETA,
b carry a pack of red flares, and
c carry a small emergency location transmitter (ELT) which automatically bleeps on the aircraft mayday frequency of 121.5 MHz.

Is your microlight suitable?

Before you fit floats take advice from someone else who has done

so, and think about the following:

a Where are your engine and propeller positioned? If they are behind you they will receive all the spray thrown up by the floats. This will rapidly wear away the propeller, and cause corrosion.
b Will your roll control (ailerons, spoilerons) be good enough to enable you to taxi without being capsized? Trikes have the same advantage here as they do on land — the entire wing can be lowered into wind.
c Is your engine powerful enough? If you are underpowered as a land-plane you will be worse off as a float-plane.

The law

In the air you are subject to air law but on the water to maritime law. You must keep clear of all other water users!

Flying on floats is delightful, but remember that:

a a microlight float-plane is more weather-sensitive than a land-plane and is much harder to taxi;

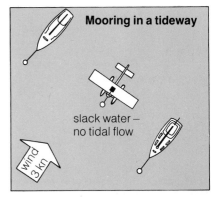

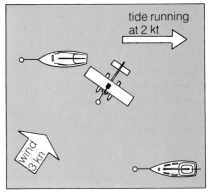

In a tideway a boat will swing with the tide much more than your microlight. If the wind now backs slightly it will collide with the boat.

b tools or cameras dropped into the water sink;
c bystanders in boats will be curious and may come too close, not realising how easily your microlight can be damaged;
d people sail boats to get away from noise, so avoid low flying or creating unnecessary noise.

15. Rallies and competitions

Club competitions and Fly-ins provide good opportunities for improving your flying and exchanging ideas and news with other pilots. The competitions, held usually over a weekend, weather permitting, will probably include precision landings and some navigational contest in which you may be given the map reference of another landing field. When you have found it and landed you are given the map reference for a further field, and so on; or you may have to observe turn point markers from the air. Such competitions are not intended to be too serious but can be thoroughly enjoyable. Most pilots take their microlights and families by car or trailer, which eliminates the need to fly home in bad weather at the end.

International competitions demand a high level of skill from the pilots, so it is worth practising first in as many local events as you have time for if you hope to be chosen for the team. The contest is likely to be based on a tour of about 500 km, made in stages over a period of up to a week and combined with additional tasks in precision landing and navigation. The winner is the pilot who gains the highest total score.

Many competitions are run with two Classes: I for trikes, and II for '3-axis' aeroplane-type microlights. International competitions are held under the auspices and rules of the *Fédération Aéronautique Internationale* and organised by different countries in turn.

Competitions not only help you to fly better but also to encourage designers to improve their aircraft. It is a recognised fact that pilots tend to buy aircraft which have performed well in big competitions.

Although some competitions

Club competitions are fun and good for your flying. Touch down as soon after flying through the gate as you can.

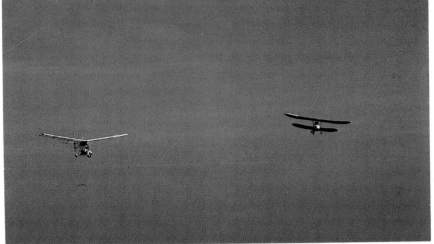

Racing is not encouraged in microlights, but an estimated elapsed time event has brought this Pipistrelle and Butterfly home together.

may not be very serious there is no point in entering unless you make some effort to succeed — if only for your own satisfaction. This means preparation.

Your aircraft

Is it in good shape? Or is it still in need of all those little jobs that you intended to do last winter? In a competition pilots will always fly in more difficult weather and a little nearer the limits than at other times, so the aircraft MUST be in top condition. There should be *nothing* waiting to be done.

Equipment

Are your maps up to date, and do they cover *all* the area over which it is possible you may fly? Is your parachute due for repacking?

If the rules require you to carry a

Coming in over a 'wall' and touching down on the spot.

This pilot has judged it well. He has cleared the 'wall' and will end up very close to the spot.

barograph:

a have you got one?

b does it work?

c how will you stow it in the aircraft? Are the organisers responsible for sealing it, or are you?

Have you got:

a tools for de-rigging, or making adjustments and replacements?

b spares for items which might cause trouble (e.g. tyres)?

c repair materials, particularly in case of fabric damage?

d a camera, films, and what about clothes, spare gloves, extra sweater?

e documents: passport, licences, logbook, insurance policy, etc.?

Have you read the competition rules, and do you understand them?

Sticking on your competition number.

If you need a retrieve-car and/or trailer, is it serviceable and does it contain its own maps, tools and other necessary equipment? Is your crew competent? Do they have passports, etc.?

This may seem to demand a great deal of work, but it will not be so if you normally look after your aircraft well and fly in a reasonably organised manner. And this depends on what sort of a pilot you are.

If you like competitions and Fly-ins you will almost certainly need a trailer. It can be a simple open trailer which is easy to load and can be used for other things at other times, or . . .

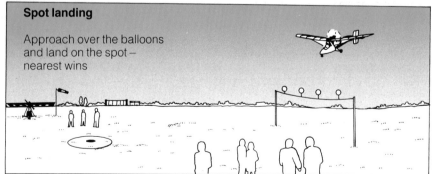

Spot landing

Approach over the balloons and land on the spot — nearest wins

Informal competitions can be fun and good practice for your flying since you may find that you are not as good as you thought you were. The 'barrier' should be light enough so that it cannot cause damage if you hit it.

Glossary and abbreviations

Aerofoil The shape of the wing section or wing profile

Ailerons Surfaces on each wing used to control roll (bank)

Airspeed Speed of an aircraft through the air

Angle of attack Angle at which the airflow arrives at the wing

Aspect ratio Ratio of wing span to the average width (chord) of the wing. In the case of a wing with varying chord, the aspect ratio is equal to: span^2/wing area

Centre of gravity (c.g.) Point on an aircraft through which the resultant force of gravity acts (balance point)

Drag Resistance to the airflow caused by the aircraft passing through the air

Elevator Horizontal surface used to control pitch. Normally it is on the tail but on a canard it is at the nose

ETA Estimated time of arrival

ETD Estimated time of departure

Glide angle (glide ratio) The distance an aircraft without power can travel horizontally for one unit of height lost

Ground effect Cushioning of the air between the wing and the ground

Groundspeed Speed of an aircraft over the ground, which varies with the wind component

Never exceed speed Speed beyond which the aircraft should not be flown (see Vne)

Pitch Rotation of an aircraft about its lateral axis (nose up or down)

QFE Altimeter set to read zero when the aircraft is on the ground at the airfield

QNH Altimeter set so that if at sea level it would read zero — it then gives altitude above sea level

Reflex Slight upward curve designed into the rear part of a wing (aerofoil) to provide pitch stability

Rudder Vertical surface(s) on the tail or at the wingtips which are used to control yaw

Roll Rotational movement of an aircraft about its longitudinal axis (left or right wing up and down)

Skid(ding) Sideways movement of the aircraft through the air, usually when too much rudder is used

Slip(ping) Sideways descending of the aircraft in the direction of the lower wingtip, usually when aircraft is turned with insufficient rudder

Spoilerons Surfaces near the wingtips, usually on the top of the wing, which can be used separately as ailerons or together as spoilers

Spoilers Surfaces, usually on the wings, which when raised increase drag and worsen the glide ratio

Stall speed Speed at which the wing no longer provides enough lift to support the weight of the aircraft

Thrust The forward action force exerted by the propeller (the *static thrust* is the thrust exerted when the aircraft is stationary)

Tip dragger(s) Vertical surfaces at the wingtips that act as rudders by increasing drag at the tip towards the direction in which the turn is to be made

Vne Maximum permitted speed; also known as *Never exceed* or *Redline*

Wind gradient Lessening of wind strength near the ground due to surface friction

Wing loading Wing area divided by the total weight of the aircraft and pilot

Yaw Rotation of an aircraft about its vertical axis (nose left or right)

Appendix 1: Organisations and addresses

British Microlight Aircraft Association
The BMAA is the national organisation which looks after microlight aviation throughout the United Kingdom. Its magazine *Flight Line* is included in the annual membership subscription (£15 p.a. in 1983). The secretary will supply information, lists of clubs and schools, etc. on request *(address:* E7 Stafford Park 4, Telford, Shropshire, TF3 3BA).

Fédération Aéronautique Internationale
Internationally, all sporting flying is looked after by the FAI, which is the world authority for the control and encouragement of records, championship organisation and rules, and pilot proficiency standards. The national aero clubs of each country are the members of FAI. The special FAI committee for microlights is the *Commission Internationale de Micro Aviation* (CIMA). Correspondence to FAI should be directed via the Royal Aero Club of the United Kingdom *(address:* Kimberley House, Vaughan Way, Leicester; *address of FAI:* 6 rue Galilée, 75782 Paris, France).

Maps and ICAO aeronautical charts
These can be bought from some flying clubs, or from Edward Stanford Ltd. (12–14 Long Acre, London WC2).

The chart of UK airspace restrictions can be obtained free from the Superintendent MoD, (procurement executive), Central Stores Depot, Aston Down, Stroud, Glos.

Civil Air Publications
From some flying clubs or from the CAA at 129 Kingsway, Holborn, London WC2.

Appendix 2: Pilot licence and FAI certificates

In the UK the microlight pilot is required by law to hold a pilot licence. This is the PPL(D) issued by the Civil Aviation Authority (CAA). It is obtained first as a Restricted licence which can with further experience be converted to an Unrestriced one. Holders of a PPL(D) are limited to the flying of microlight aircraft. The licence is permanent but has to be kept current by flying at least 5 hours in each period of 13 months, not more than 2 hours being dual. The medical declaration of fitness countersigned by a doctor also has to be revalidated every 2 years for a pilot under 40 and annually thereafter. Details in the CAA publication CAP 53 (1983 edition).

The Restricted PPL(D)

The holder of a Restricted licence may fly only within 8 nautical miles of his take-off place, by day, and in reasonable weather. He may not carry passengers. The requirements are that the pilot must:

1 hold a valid medical certificate
2 have reached the age of 17 years
3 produce logbook evidence of not less than 15 hours' flying of which at least 7 must be solo, and include a 25 km triangular flight made within a radius of 8 nautical miles of the airfield.
4 have been trained to a CAA approved syllabus by a Group D rated instructor.
5 pass ground exams on navigation, meterology, air law, and the microlight.
6 pass a flight test conducted or supervised by an examiner authorised by CAA.
7 pay the licence fee to CAA (£45 in 1983).

The Unrestricted PPL(D)

To convert the Restricted licence to unrestricted the pilot must:

1 obtain 5 hours' navigation training from a qualified instructor: 3 hours at least must be solo and must include two 75 km triangular cross-country flights with authorised outlandings.
2 have built up a total of 25 hours' flying. There is no charge for converting the licence. The pilot may now carry a passenger.

The FAI Colibri Proficiency Badges

In addition to the mandatory licence a microlight pilot can work for international proficiency standards to improve his skills. The Bronze, Silver and Gold Colibri badges are recognisable all over the world and will increasingly be used as entry levels for international competitions. The Bronze Colibri has similar requirements to the PPL(D) so a pilot holding an Unrestricted licence should be able to obtain it easily. The requirements are:

Bronze

a 20 hours solo on microlight aircraft including at least 50 logged flights.
b 3 Precision landings within 10 m of the centre of a given spot.
c 1 Precision landing within 20 m of the centre of a given spot from a height of 300 m (1000 ft) AGL with the throttle fully closed. Demonstrations of correct go-around (overshoot) procedure.
d Two 75 km cross-country flights over a triangular course, one with an outlanding at a designated point along the route.

Silver

a 100 hours on microlight aircraft including at least 200 logged flights.

b 2 flights to approx. 300 m (1000 ft) AGL, stop engine(s), complete a 360° turn and land within 5 m of the centre of a given spot.
c Four 150 km cross-country flights with any landing or turn points pre-declared. The courses may be straight, dog-leg (1 turn point), out and return, or triangular (2 turn points).

Gold

a 300 hours on microlight aircraft.
b Have competed in 2 National or International microlight competitions conducted in accordance with FAI rules.
c Complete a tour of at least 500 km in length flight plan within 7 consecutive days. The route to contain at least 3 control points which the aircraft is observed to overfly or where a landing is made. Only the final landing of the tour may be made at the initial departure point.
d Hold one of the following: (1) National microlight instructor rating. (2) National microlight record (or have held such a record). (3) National microlight seaplane rating plus two 75 km cross-country flights on a seaplane. (4) National Alpine rating.

Appendix 3: Units and conversions

Aviation has not done too well in simplifying the problem of mixing different units. Distance can be measured in nautical miles or kilometres, speed in knots (1 knot = 1 nautical mile per hour) or kilometres per hour, and height in feet or metres. If you are familiar with both systems, so much the better, but if not the table below should help you make any necessary conversions.

It is useful to remember that 1 knot equals approximately 100 ft/min
1 knot = 0.515 m/s
1 m/s = 1.94 knots

Length
1 foot (ft) = 0.305 m
1 inch (in) = 25.4 mm
0.001 in (1 'thou') = 0.025 mm
(25 microns)
1 metre (m) = 3.28 ft
1 millimetre (mm) = 0.0394 in
(= approx. 40 'thou')

Area
1 ft^2 = 0.0929 m^2
1 m^2 = 10.76 ft^2

Volume
1 in^3 = 16.38 cm^3
1 cm^3 (1 cc) = 0.0612 in^3

Weight
1 pound (lb) = 0.454 kg
1 kilogram (kg) = 2.205 lb

Wing loading
1 lb/ft^2 = 4.88 kg/m^2
1 kg/m^2 = 0.205 lb/ft^2

Fuel capacity

Imperial Gal (used in UK) Gal*		U.S. Gallon U.S. Gal**		Litre l
1	=	1.20	=	4.54
0.833	=	1	=	3.78
0.220	=	0.264	=	1

* Divided into 4 quarts or 8 pints   ** Divided into 4 US quarts or 8 US pints

Weights of fuel (specific gravity = 0.73)

Unit	Wt. (lb)	Wt. (kg)
Imperial gallon	7.3	3.31
US gallon	6.08	2.76
Litre	1.61	0.73

Appendix 4: Air law

The Air Law which the microlight pilot must know is contained in the *Air Navigation Order (ANO)*, the *Air Pilot, The Aeronautical Information Publication (AIP)* and *NOTAMS.* All are available from CAA.

Before any pilot begins to fly across country on his own he must learn about the many regulations which will affect him — including ground signals and lights, visual distress signals, the carriage of dangerous goods, drunkenness in aircraft, notification of accidents, and most importantly, about where he may or may not fly.

Controlled airspace
This includes: CONTROL ZONES (areas which extend from the surface upwards to a defined level); CONTROL AREAS (these start from a defined level and extend upwards to a further defined level); AIRWAYS (corridors of controlled airspace linking major airports). A *purple airway* is a temporary airway for the passage of royal flights. For all practical purposes a microlight may not enter controlled airspace without permission.

Prohibited areas
Atomic Energy Establishment areas have a radius of 2 nautical miles and extend 2,000

feet upwards. *Danger Areas* are used for military firing, including the use of pilotless target aircraft. Although it is not always an offence to enter them it may be extremely unwise. *Restricted or hazardous areas* include almost anything from high-intensity radio transmission areas, free-fall parachute areas and bird sanctuaries.

Aerodrome traffic zones
Every aerodrome has a traffic zone (ATZ), extending from the surface to 2,000 feet within 1.5 nautical miles of the airfield boundaries, which may not be entered without permission. Some aerodromes also have a special rules zone (SRZ). All aircraft have to conform to air traffic control (ATC) instructions while within the area. Some military aerodromes have a traffic zone (MATZ), which has a 5 nautical mile radius with a projecting stub 4 miles wide aligned with the main approach and extending to 3,000 feet. A civil aircraft need only observe the standard ATC.

VFR and IFR
All flights must be conducted in accordance with either Visual Flight Rules (VFR) or Instrument Flight Rules (IFR). Unless it is specially equipped to operate IFR, the microlight must fly VFR. Visual Meteorological Conditions (VMC) are those which enable the pilot to maintain VFR. Briefly, they are:
a *Above 3,000 ft.* Remain 1 n.m. horizontally and 1,000 ft vertically from cloud, and in a flight visibility of at least 5 n.m.
b *Below 3,000 ft.* If flying at less than 140 knots, clear of cloud, in sight of the surface and in a flight visibility of at least 1 n.m.
Instrument Meteorological Conditions (IMC) are those when the pilot cannot comply with VMC.
The Air Law requirements are given in CAP 85, issued by CAA.

Appendix 5: ICAO standard atmosphere

Altitude	Temperature		Pressure	
ft	°C	°F	mb	in Hg
0	15.00	59.0	1013.2	29.92
1000	13.02	55.4	997.2	28.86
2000	11.04	51.9	942.1	27.82
3000	9.06	48.3	908.1	26.82
4000	7.08	44.7	875.1	25.84
5000	5.10	41.2	843.1	24.90
6000	3.11	37.6	812.0	23.98
7000	+ 1.13	34.0	781.9	23.09
8000	− 0.85	30.5	752.6	22.22
9000	− 2.83	26.9	724.3	21.39
10000	− 4.81	23.3	696.8	20.58
15000	−14.72	+ 5.5	571.8	16.89
20000	−24.62	−12.3	465.6	13.75
25000	−34.53	−30.2	376.0	11.10

Appendix 6: ICAO alphabet

A Alpha
B Bravo
C Charlie
D Delta
E Echo
F Foxtrot
G Golf
H Hotel
I India
J Juliet
K Kilo

L Lima
M Mike
N November
O Oscar
P Papa
Q Quebec
R Romeo
S Sierra
T Tango
U Uniform
V Victor

W Whiskey
X X-ray
Y Yankee
Z Zulu

Bibliography

Microlight Aircraft and the Air, Brian Cosgrove (from BMAA), 1982.
Flight Briefing for Microlight Pilots, Birch and Bramson, Pitman, 1983.
Pilot's Weather, Ann Welch, John Murray, 1978.
Ultralight and Microlight Aircraft of the World, Berger and Burr, Haynes, 1983.